Global & UK Poverty

Series Editor: Cara Acred

Volume 306

D1081342

Independence Educational Publishers

First published by Independence Educational Publishers

The Studio, High Green

Great Shelford

Cambridge CB22 5EG

England

© Independence 2016

ISBN-13: 978 1 86168 751 7

Printed in Great Britain
Zenith Print Group

Contents

Introduction

Global & UK Poverty is Volume 306 in the **ISSUES** series. The aim of the series is to offer current, diverse information about important issues in our world, from a UK perspective.

ABOUT GLOBAL & UK POVERTY

Today, 3.7 million children in the UK are living in poverty and, despite reaching the end of the Millennium Development Goals, global poverty remains a deeply worrying issue. This book explores poverty in the UK and around the globe. It looks at the impact poverty has on individuals and families, exploring topics such as the rise of food banks and the link between poverty and mental health. It also considers what can be done to eradicate poverty, once and for all.

OUR SOURCES

Titles in the **ISSUES** series are designed to function as educational resource books, providing a balanced overview of a specific subject.

The information in our books is comprised of facts, articles and opinions from many different sources, including:

⇨ Newspaper reports and opinion pieces

⇨ Website factsheets

⇨ Magazine and journal articles

⇨ Statistics and surveys

⇨ Government reports

⇨ Literature from special interest groups.

A NOTE ON CRITICAL EVALUATION

Because the information reprinted here is from a number of different sources, readers should bear in mind the origin of the text and whether the source is likely to have a particular bias when presenting information (or when conducting their research). It is hoped that, as you read about the many aspects of the issues explored in this book, you will critically evaluate the information presented.

It is important that you decide whether you are being presented with facts or opinions. Does the writer give a biased or unbiased report? If an opinion is being expressed, do you agree with the writer? Is there potential bias to the 'facts' or statistics behind an article?

ASSIGNMENTS

In the back of this book, you will find a selection of assignments designed to help you engage with the articles you have been reading and to explore your own opinions. Some tasks will take longer than others and there is a mixture of design, writing and research-based activities that you can complete alone or in a group.

FURTHER RESEARCH

At the end of each article we have listed its source and a website that you can visit if you would like to conduct your own research. Please remember to critically evaluate any sources that you consult and consider whether the information you are viewing is accurate and unbiased.

Useful weblinks

www.actionaid.org.uk

www.actionforchildren.org.uk

www.barnardos.org.uk

www.childrenssociety.org

www.childrenssociety.org.uk

www.cpag.org.uk

www.dosomething.org

www.equalitytrust.org.uk

www.foodethicscouncil.org

www.heraldscotland.com

www.huffingtonpost.co.uk

www.independent.co.uk

www.jrf.org.uk

www.lankellychase.org.uk

www.londonspovertyprofile.org

www.northumbria.ac.uk

www.npi.org.uk

www.ryantunnardbrown.com

www.societycentral.ac.uk

sustainabledevelopment.un.org

www.telegraph.co.uk

www.theconversation.com

www.theguardian.com

www.trusselltrust.org

www.weforum.org

www.welfareweekly.com

www.wfp.org

www.who.int

What is poverty?

When we think about poverty, many of us recall TV images from the developing world: of famine, of shanty towns, or of children dying from preventable diseases. Yet this is clearly not what we observe in the UK.

So is there any poverty in the UK?

Peter Townsend, the sociologist who did so much to advance our understanding of poverty and its relationship to wider society, and was also one of the founders of the Child Poverty Action Group (CPAG), certainly thought so. In 1979 Townsend defined poverty as follows:

"Individuals, families and groups in the population can be said to be in poverty when they lack resources to obtain the type of diet, participate in the activities and have the living conditions and amenities which are customary, or at least widely encouraged and approved, in the societies in which they belong."[1]

As this definition makes clear, in affluent societies such as the UK poverty can only properly be understood in relation to the typical living standards in society.

Townsend's definition also highlights that poverty is about a lack of resources. Poor people lack capital (both income and wealth). But they can also be resource-poor in other ways: they may lack human capital (such as education or good health), or social capital (such as positive and trustful communities). Yet it is money that, to a large extent, determines whether people are able to compensate for other shortfalls in their lives. That is why a lack of adequate financial resources is the decisive characteristic of poverty.

And as the information in this article shows, poverty is indeed a fact of life for many living in the UK today.

Measuring poverty

Measuring poverty is not just a technical exercise. What we decide to measure is informed by our understanding of poverty. In turn, this determines what we think are the correct policy responses required to end poverty.

Income

Although poverty is about more than just money, the most widely used poverty measure in the UK is household income. It is reasonably easy to collect, and to compare across time and countries.

In addition, while there are legitimate criticisms one can make of certain income measures, they do capture the essential truth that, in the modern world, an adequate amount of money is needed to participate fully in society.

Consumption

Some view consumption as a better measure of poverty than income. A recent IFS study has shown, for example, that those on the reported lowest incomes do not always coincide with the group with the lowest spending habits, or those living in the severest forms of deprivation.[2]

Consumption data has its limitations however: it is harder to collect than information on income, and is more prone to error. In addition, while consumption measures map low levels of living, they are silent about the resources needed to avoid them.

Material deprivation

Other studies suggest that material deprivation can usefully complement other poverty measures.[3] Material deprivation captures the consequences of long-term poverty on families rather than the immediate financial strain that they experience. It recognises that such families are not able to afford certain possessions most of us take for granted, or are unable to replace worn out items.

While such measures do provide valuable information, however, they risk restricting poverty to those already suffering its long-term consequences.

Wellbeing

In recent years composite measures of wellbeing have been developed which aim to capture the multi-dimensionality of poverty. For example, in 2007 UNICEF issued a report card on child wellbeing in rich countries, which brought together information on material conditions with other indicators such as health, education, peer and family relationships, behaviours and risks, and young people's own subjective sense of wellbeing.[4]

Such studies provide us with a rich picture of life experiences, but conflating wellbeing with poverty is misleading. Critically, multi-dimensional accounts of poverty marginalise financial resources, the lack of which is the essential feature of poverty.

2 M Brewer et al, *The living standards of families with children reporting low incomes*, Institute for Fiscal Studies, 2009

3 See, for example, M Willitts, *Measuring child poverty using material deprivation: Possible approaches*, DWP Working Paper 28, Department for Work and Pensions, 2006

4 UNICEF, *Child poverty in perspective: An overview of child wellbeing in rich countries*, UNICEF, 2007

1 P Townsend, *Poverty in the United Kingdom*, Allen Lane, 1979

The UK poverty line

Each year, the Government publishes a survey of income poverty in the UK called *Households below average income* (HBAI).

This survey sets the poverty line in the UK at 60 per cent of the median UK household income. In other words, if a household's income is less than 60 per cent of this average, HBAI considers them to be living in poverty.

Before or after housing costs?

HBAI provides two types of household data: before housing costs are deducted (BHC) and after housing costs have been removed (AHC). Many official poverty statistics employ the BHC information. CPAG considers a better measure to be the income a household has left AHC, as this more realistically reflects the amount of money families and individuals have at their disposal. All the figures we use are AHC unless otherwise stated.

Adjustments made to HBAI

The HBAI poverty line takes into account the size and the composition of households through a process called equivalisation. As common sense would suggest, the poverty line for a household with one adult and one child is set at a lower level than a two parent family with more children.

The poverty line is not adjusted, however, for other important household characteristics such as disability or caring responsibilities.

How much?

The table below shows the HBAI poverty line for 2014 to 2015, for a couple and a lone parent with two children, excluding housing costs.

Family composition		
	Per month	**Per year**
Lone parent (2 children)	£1,261	£15,132
Couple (2 children)	£1,703	£20,436

⇨ The above information is reprinted with kind permission from the Child Poverty Action Group (CPAG). Please visit www.cpag.org.uk for further information.

© CPAG 2000–2016

The scale of economic inequality in the UK

UK income inequality

The UK has a very high level of income inequality compared to other developed countries.

Households in the bottom 10% of the population have on average a net income of £9,277. The top 10% have net incomes over nine times that (£83,897). As can be seen from the graph, income inequality is much starker at the top of the income scale, with the group with the ninth highest incomes making only 60% of the top 10%'s income. Inequality is much higher amongst original income than net income with the poorest 10% having on average an original income of £4,467 whilst the top 10% have an original income 24 times larger (£107,597).[1]

Differences within the top 1%

The top 1% have incomes substantially higher than the rest of those in the top 10%. In 2012, the top 1% had an average income of £253,927 and the top 0.1% had an average income of £919,882.[2]

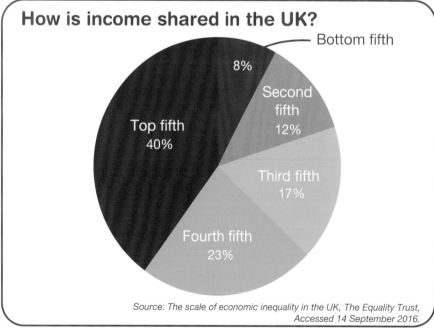

How is income shared in the UK?

- Bottom fifth 8%
- Second fifth 12%
- Third fifth 17%
- Fourth fifth 23%
- Top fifth 40%

Source: The scale of economic inequality in the UK, The Equality Trust, Accessed 14 September 2016.

1 Mean household income, original and net, 2014-15 ONS

2 World Top Incomes Database

How income is shared

The poorest fifth of society have only 8% of the total income, whereas the top fifth have 40%.

Income spread between the UK's regions and nations

Income is also spread unequally across the UK's regions and nations. The average household income in London is considerably higher than in the North East.

GB wealth inequality

Wealth in Great Britain is even more unequally divided than income. The richest 10% of households hold 45% of all wealth. The poorest 50%, by contrast, own just 8.7%.[3]

Wealth spread between Great Britain's regions and nations

Wealth is also unevenly spread across Great Britain. An average household in the South East has almost twice (183%) the amount of wealth of an average household in Scotland.[4]

How does the UK compare to other countries?

Wealth

Compared to the other OECD countries, the UK has a relatively equal distribution of wealth. The UK has a wealth GINI coefficient of 67.8% compared to an OECD average of 71.8%.

Income

Compared to other developed countries, the UK has a very unequal distribution of income. Out of the 30 OECD countries in the LIS data set, the UK is the joint sixth most unequal, and within this data set it is the third most unequal in Europe.[5]

Updated August 2016

⇨ The above information is reprinted with kind permission from The Equality Trust. Please visit www.equalitytrust.org.uk for further information.

3 Household, 2012-2014 ONS

4 Household, 2012-2014 ONS

5 Luxembourg Income Study

Here's what we learned from mapping out England's inequalities

An article from **The Conversation.**

THE CONVERSATION

By Alasdair Rae, Senior Lecturer in Urban Studies and Planning, University of Sheffield

With its long history of feudal oppression, industrial workhouses and dire slums, England is no stranger to deprivation. Even today, we're all too familiar with phenomena like 'beds in sheds', soaring food bank use and fuel poverty. So it's hardly surprising that, whenever a new deprivation data set is released, we tend to focus our attention on the 'most deprived' places across England.

While these areas warrant urgent attention, there are also many other significant stories to be told. So, when the Government released the latest *Indices of Deprivation* for England, I delved into the data through mapping and analysis to see what I could uncover. But before I share my findings, it will be helpful to explain what deprivation actually is.

Deprivation is measured based on a mix of indicators relating to income, jobs, education, health, crime, housing and environment. It's a broader measure than poverty – which tends to focus on income – but there is significant overlap between the two.

By combining deprivation data from 2010 and 2015 with freely available map data, I produced deprivation maps for all 326 of England's local authorities – all of which are available for download and re-use on my website. The overall message is clear: not much has changed.

For example, 49% of Middlesbrough's neighbourhoods remain within the most deprived 10% in England, compared to 47% in 2010. It's a similar story in Hull, where 45% were in England's most deprived decile in 2015, compared to 43% in 2010.

Unlike poverty, deprivation is a relative measure, which means that we can also locate England's 'least deprived' areas – such as Hart, in Hampshire. Yet the patterns in these areas have also proved to be very persistent: not much has changed at either end of the deprivation spectrum.

Of course, this persistence shouldn't surprise us. We're only talking about a five-year period – and even the most optimistic policymaker wouldn't expect much to change in half a decade. In fact, they probably wouldn't expect to see much change over a whole decade, so entrenched are patterns of deprivation and so humble the impacts of urban policy.

A special case

But there is one major exception to this rule: London. If we map out the data from the 2004 *Indices of Deprivation*, and compare them to the most recent results, we see some striking changes.

I looked at areas in London which were within England's most deprived decile in both 2004 and 2015. In 2004, London had 462 of England's 10% most deprived areas. By 2015, this figure had shrunk to 274.

The disappearance of many of the red areas since 2004 helps document the apparent dispersal of London's poorest residents over little more than a decade.

These changes are most obvious in areas at the forefront of gentrification struggles, such as Tower Hamlets, Hackney, Newham and Camden.

Hold on a minute though. Shouldn't we be applauding the elimination of London's most deprived areas? If these changes were due to individuals escaping deprivation and poverty, then the answer would be "yes". But I don't believe this is the case.

Given the influx of new residents in these areas, it's more likely to be a result of changing local populations, particularly in East London where the process of gentrification is well documented. As recent events like the Cereal Killer Cafe protests have shown, this inevitably results in conflict and resentment at a local level.

At the same time, we are also seeing increases in the number of deprived neighbourhoods in some Outer London Boroughs, such as Bromley. The two phenomena may not be directly related, but I wouldn't rule it out. It could well be that as wealthier residents move into the more central boroughs, poorer Londoners are being pushed toward the city's more affordable outskirts.

If we're serious about tackling acute deprivation in our society, then we should shift our focus beyond deprivation and towards inequality itself. Thankfully, the realisation is gradually dawning that addressing inequalities on a national level should be a matter of priority. The OECD has argued that when inequality rises,

economic growth falls – and that we should all be more concerned with how those on the bottom 40% of incomes in society fare.

Yet this message has to date had little impact upon government policies around the globe. To address the kinds of inequalities seen in England, there first needs to be a realisation that the impacts of austerity policies tend to be very spatially uneven and often serve to intensify levels of deprivation at the local level. This message isn't currently a popular one, but I think it needs urgent attention.

14 October 2015

⇨ The above information is reprinted with kind permission from *The Conversation*. Please visit www.theconversation.com for further information.

© 2010–2016, The Conversation Trust (UK)

Material deprivation rates for different groups of those in families with children by income poverty status, 2012–13 to 2014–15 (UK)		
	Material deprivation rate	
	In income poverty	**Not in income poverty**
Household work status		
Someone in work	33%	10%
No one in work	64%	53%
Number of adults		
Lone-parent household	59%	34%
Not lone-parent household	38%	9%
Disability		
Someone in household disabled	59%	25%
No one in household disabled	36%	9%
Ethnicity		
All adults in household are white	41%	11%
At least one adult is non-white	51%	21%
All	20%	

Note: Incomes have been measured net of taxes and benefits and after housing costs have been deducted. The poverty line is 60% of 2010–11 AHC median income.

Source: Authors' calculations using the Family Resources Survey, 2012–13, 2013–14 and 2014–15.

Multiple disadvantage timeline

Looking back over history tells us that the habit of thinking about disadvantage in terms of discrete single issues is as old as time – and so it is no surprise that this is how people continue to be portrayed. This is necessarily a brief timeline – a complete history would be a huge project in its own right.

900 AD – First almshouses established

Almshouses, the ancestor of today's hostels for the homeless, grew out of the monastic obligation to provide lodgings for those in need, and were established in England in the 10th Century, with the first recorded almshouse founded by King Athelstan in York. The word "hospital" derives from these almshouses that sheltered the sick and needy, although that word dates from rather later, the mid 14th century, and also subsequently gave modern English the word "hostel".

1247 – Bethlem Hospital

Europe's oldest psychiatric hospital, Bethlem, now part of South London and Maudsley NHS foundation, was founded in 1247 by Christians to provide shelter for the homeless, and over time became known as a place for the mad. Originally known as the Priory of St Mary of Bethlehem, its name contracted over time to Bedlam as it became a "hospital for the insane". While the hospital nowadays is a renowned centre of excellence for the mentally ill, the old stigma lives on in the word "bedlam", which survives to this day.

1388 – Poor Law Act

The Black Death of the mid 14th century killed around a third of the population, causing dramatic labour shortages, which a 1388 amendment to the Poor Law sought to address by restricting the movement of workers: servants who wanted to be moved needed written permission to do so, while beggars could no longer pretend to be itinerant labourers. That in turn meant that parishes had to assume responsibility for the poor, leading eventually to the introduction of workhouses.

1536 – Punishment of Sturdy Vagabonds and Beggars Henry VII

By 1536, the year Henry VIII had Anne Boleyn executed, the need to provide for the poor had become a pressing problem. This act compelled local officials to ensure that the poor in their parishes did not need to beg. However, it prohibited levying a compulsory tax to provide funds, so parish officials instead organised collections to fund relief, while "sturdy vagabonds" could be set to work by local authorities after having been punished. This act is a watershed as it marks the start of considering whether to pay for the poor out of taxation.

1741 – Foundling Hospital for Orphans established

The growth of empire saw a mass movement of people into the booming cities – and a rise in child mortality and abandonment: children were routinely shunted into prisons or workhouses, or even hastened to their demise with a dose of opium and treacle. As a response to the growing problem, philanthropist Thomas Coram set up the Foundling Hospital, the UK's first children's charity. The establishment of Coram's hospital was part of a wave of philanthropy, and Coram's hospital in particular became London's most popular charity. More importantly, Coram set a standard and a framework for this kind of charitable enterprise – and the charity survives to this day, helping more than 1m children and young people every year.

1834 – New Poor Law

The old system of poor relief was under pressure by the end of the Georgian era and the start of Queen Victoria's reign thanks to the Industrial Revolution, which caused a sharp rise in unemployment, and a series of bad harvests. An endowment to the Poor Law Act aimed to reduce the cost of providing for the poor, and for the first time introduced a role for central government. A key point of this law, which echoes today, is that it compelled the poor to support themselves by working in return for shelter and education for their children in the workhouse.

1908 – Children's Charter

The early 1900s saw the establishment of juvenile courts. Local authorities were given powers to keep children out of the workhouse, preventing them from working in dangerous trades. Among other things, it also prevented children from purchasing cigarettes and entering pubs and eventually led to councils setting up social services and Orphanages.

1918-1939 – The inter-war years

A period of consolidation and progressive thought towards the vulnerable in society. Courts were required to regard a child's welfare, the age of criminal of responsibility was raised to eight years old, and the death penalty was abolished for teens. In 1920, Britain's first formal drug legislation was passed - The Dangerous Drugs Act - significantly shifting power from the Ministry of Health to the Home Office in this field.

1940s and 1950s – The Post-war period

Widely regarded as a period of formalization of the modern British welfare state, post-war Britain was seen by many as an opportunity to improve the lives of the population. Many Britons lived in a state of poverty and there was a shortage of quality houses. William Beveridge, author of the 1942 Beveridge Report and Liberal politician, identified five issues that needed to be tackled "on the road to reconstruction" - poverty; disease; ignorance; squalor and idleness.

Outlining a network of social care for the individual 'from cradle to grave', the report paved the way for working age income support system, child benefit, a public housing scheme and the creation of the National Health Service (1948). This new build policy continued when the Conservative Party came to power in 1951, with 3 million new houses being built in Britain during the 1950s.

1960s and 1970s – Economic Growth; Civil Rights and Equality movements

A time of sustained economic growth and Britain reaching near full employment in the 1970s, leading to higher tax revenues and falling debt to GDP. However, by the late 1960s services for people facing disadvantage were increasingly discrete in their nature. For example, housing and homelessness was viewed as a problem facing single people and so separated from children's and youth services and domestic abuse was barely tackled by the state.

The 1970s witnessed equality and civil rights movements across much of Europe and North America. In Britain, anti-discrimination laws primarily aimed at women and people from minority backgrounds were introduced including the Equal Pay Act (1970) the Sex Discrimination Act (1975) and the Race Relations Act (1976). These were seminal pieces of legislation, but programmatic response tended to be fractured with limited co-ordination across services and largely reliant on the voluntary sector with unreliable funding sources. Critically, there was no concept of 'generalised disadvantage'.

1980s and 1990s – Rising Inequality

Mass redundancies, strikes and major industrial conflicts were typical aspects of 1980s Britain, characterised as the 'sick man of Europe'. According to the Institute for Fiscal Studies, poverty increased under Thatcher by 8.8 % from 1979 to 1990 and with it came inequality. However, public spending as a percentage of GDP actually rose in the Conservative government's first years of power, before going down.

By the mid 1990s, Britain was experiencing chronic levels of social disadvantage and inequality. The New Labour government set out an ambitious vision to end social exclusion as part of a project to re-build Britain as 'one nation, in which each citizen has a stake'. In 1997, the Social Exclusion Unit (SEU) was launched as part of the Cabinet Office as a response to governments trying "to deal with each of the problems of social exclusion individually" and aimed to produce "joined-up solutions to joined-up problems". The unit was abolished in 2010.

The above information is reprinted with kind permission from Lankelly Chase. Please visit www.lankellychase.org.uk for further information.

Ten of top 12 most declining UK cities are in north of England – report

Joseph Rowntree Foundation study puts Rochdale, Burnley and Bolton at top of list of cities faring worst compared with UK trends.

By Frances Perraudin

Ten of the top 12 most declining UK cities are in the north of England, a report says, prompting calls for the Government to ensure its devolution agenda does not only benefit big northern cities.

A study from the Joseph Rowntree Foundation (JRF) analysed the fortunes of 74 UK cities with populations of more than 100,000, developing an index of relative decline based on changes in employment rates, levels of highly qualified workers, the number and type of full-time jobs, net migration rates and population change.

Rochdale, Burnley and Bolton topped the list of cities that have fared the worst compared with national trends, and Hull and Grimsby were at five and six. No city in the south of England featured in the top 24 of the index.

Researchers from the Centre for Urban and Regional Development Studies at Newcastle University, which conducted the study along with the JRF, said George Osborne should ensure all parts of the north benefited from his "northern powerhouse" project.

The project aims to boost economic growth in the north of England – particularly the "core cities" of Liverpool, Manchester, Leeds, Sheffield and Newcastle – and rebalance the UK economy away from London and the South East, partly by devolving political power to northern regions. The researchers said their report demonstrated the need for areas outside the biggest cities to share the benefits of investment and devolution.

Andy Pike, co-author of the report and professor of local and regional development at Newcastle University, said: "Economic and social conditions in UK cities are diverging and increasingly different. Many cities in the north are growing but are failing to keep up with national trends."

He added: "If the commitment to rebalancing in the UK is meaningful then greater policy attention and resources by central and local government needs to be focused upon the particular needs of these cities lagging behind."

Josh Stott, policy and research manager at JRF, said: "Britain has the potential to become a more prosperous country, with George Osborne's northern powerhouse playing a key role in rebalancing the economy. But it must reach all parts of the north to ensure prosperity is shared.

"To rebalance the economy and ensure local growth provides opportunity for all households, the Treasury needs to ensure areas outside of core cities are not left behind. City leaders – with a new suite of powers at their disposal – must also show leadership to do their part to ensure growth and prosperity is shared by all."

29 February 2016

⇨ The above information is reprinted with kind permission from *The Guardian*. Please visit www.theguardian.com for further information.

London's poverty profile

Key facts

⇨ 27% of Londoners live in poverty after housing costs are taken into account, compared with 20% in the rest of England. The cost of housing is an important factor in London's higher poverty rate.

⇨ The majority of people living in poverty are in a working family. As employment has increased so has the number of people in a working family in poverty – from 700,000 to 1.2 million in the last decade, an increase of 70%.

⇨ The total wealth of a household at the bottom (the 10th percentile) is £6,300; towards the top (the 90th percentile) it was £1.1 million. London's 90:10 wealth ratio is 173, almost three times the ratio for the rest of Britain (at 60).

⇨ The number of unemployed adults is at its lowest level since 2008, at just over 300,000. The unemployment ratio in Inner London has halved over the past 20 years reaching 5.6%, slightly higher than Outer London (5.2%) and the rest of England (4.8%).

⇨ Almost 700,000 jobs in London (18%) pay below the London Living Wage. This number has increased for five consecutive years, particularly among men working full-time.

⇨ At 860,000 there are more people in poverty in private rented housing than there are in social rented or owner-occupied homes. A decade ago it was the least common tenure among those in poverty.

⇨ The vast majority of children in poverty are in rented housing (more than 530,000), half with a registered social landlord and half with a private landlord. The number of children in poverty in private rented housing has more than doubled in ten years.

⇨ In the three years to 2013/14 there was a net increase of 7,700 affordable homes a year compared with a target of 13,200, meaning the target was missed by 40%. 60% of these new homes were available for social rent.

⇨ In 2014/15 there were 27,000 landlord possession orders (permitting landlords to immediately evict tenants). This rate is more than double the rest of England. The highest rates were in Outer London.

⇨ 48,000 households live in temporary accommodation in London (three times higher than the rest of England put together), 15,600 of which live outside their home borough. Over the last two years an estimated 2,700 families have been placed in accommodation outside London.

⇨ In 2015, 10,500 families were affected by the overall benefit cap including 2,400 losing more than £100 per week. If the cap is lowered as planned, they will lose another £58 a week and a further 20,000 families will be affected.

⇨ Half of 0- to 19-year-olds in London (1.1. million) live in a family that receives tax credits. 640,000 children benefit from in-work tax credits and are likely to be worse off when these are cut in April 2016.

⇨ In every London borough pupils receiving free school meals performed better on average at GCSE than their peers in the rest of England.

⇨ The above information is reprinted with kind permission from London's Poverty Profile. Please visit www.londonspovertyprofile.org for further information.

The population of London's sub-regions

	Total population (millions)	Population increase in last decade	People per square km	%BME*	% not UK-born
Inner East & South	2.3	21%	10,800	48%	41%
Inner West	1.1	7%	10,400	32%	44%
Outer East & Northeast	1.8	15%	4,300	37%	29%
Outer South	1.3	10%	3,600	30%	25%
Outer West & Northwest	2.0	15%	4,400	46%	42%
London	8.5	15%	5,400	40%	37%
Rest of England	45.8	7%	400	10%	10%

*BME (Black and minority ethic) refers to all non-white ethnic groups.

Source: ONS mid-year population estimates for 2004 and 2014, ONS; ethnic minority and non-UK-born from Census 2011.

© London's Poverty Profile 2016

4.7 million people cannot afford to keep the lights on

Nearly five million people in fuel poverty cannot afford to keep the lights on and pay energy bills, according to new research published today.

Research by the Debt Advisory Centre found that 4.7 million people across the UK are frequently cut off from their electricity supply, because they cannot afford to top-up pre-paid electricity meters.

Pre-paid meters are usually more expensive than other payment options, but fuel poor households say they rely on them to better manage energy costs.

Around 25% of families across the UK rely on pre-paid meters to help pay energy bills, with one in ten saying they are in arrears with gas, water or electricity.

18% of households questioned by the Debt Advisory Centre said their gas supply is cut off on average every few months, while 7% were left without gas at least once per week.

Around 6% of respondents said they were regularly left without electricity at least once a week.

Households in the West Midlands and East Midlands have the highest rates of fuel poverty, with 63% of those in the East Midlands struggling to afford to top-up pre-paid meters.

Fuel poverty is defined as households who spend more than 10% of the overall income on fuel and energy costs.

A Debt Advisory Centre spokesperson said: "To see this level of fuel poverty in the UK is very worrying. Heating, lighting and hot water are basic necessities that everyone should have access to, yet there are many vulnerable households who are forced to go without.

"We would like to see more help given to households in danger of losing their energy supply.

"Fuel poverty is defined as households who spend more than 10% of the overall income on fuel and energy costs"

"I would advise anyone whose energy is at risk of being cut-off to speak to their supplier as soon as possible to ask for help, and also, to contact the Home Heat Helpline for free advice on getting out of fuel poverty.

"The Debt Advisory Centre would also like to see those customers who are able to demonstrate that they can pay energy bills to be taken off pre-paid meters and put on to cheaper deals."

Energy giant npower recently announced the creation of a fuel voucher scheme for families struggling with energy costs. Dubbed "fuel banks" by critics, vouchers will be made available through Trussell Trust food banks.

The scheme is open to all families struggling with energy costs and not just npower customers or pre-paid meter users.

Last edited at 6:17pm on 13/05/2015. Correction: The Debt Advisory Centre is a debt advice and solutions provider and not a registered charity.

⇨ The above information is reprinted with kind permission from Welfare Weekly. Please visit www.welfareweekly.com for further information.

Poverty: the real story?

A new report tells the stories of 20 people living in poverty, struggling against the odds – as well as hardening attitudes and a lack of understanding of their lives – and calls urgently for change.

Sally's unemployed son Chris lives with her in the Midlands. They both live on benefits. Sally is an activist with an anti-poverty organisation. Chris was sanctioned for being late for an appointment with his private sector Work Programme advisor. Road works slowed the bus down, and he had run out of credit on his mobile so could not ring to let them know. The decision by the Jobcentre to sanction him was taken on the basis of DNA – 'did not attend'. He won his case on appeal – but only a long time after Sally had supported him on her benefits for the month he had no Jobseeker's Allowance.

Jenny has long-standing health problems and severe learning difficulties. She has managed her benefits money well for many years. But recently she has been under pressure from her bank because of an overdraft, taken out years ago by her former husband, for which she is now liable (though she never used the account herself). The overdraft was small originally, but it has crept up over the limit and now incurs interest as well as fees and penalty charges. Over the years she has asked how she can settle the debt but no one has suggested she close the account to arrange a repayment plan. She is now getting advice, but the bank wants its money back.

These are just two out of 20 people's stories from a new report, *Our lives: Challenging attitudes to poverty in 2015*. The report was written by a group of women who have spent most of their lives living and working closely with families and communities grappling with poverty. We wrote it as a result of a direct challenge issued by Bob Holman, an ex-academic activist from Easterhouse, in an article in *The Guardian*.

Bob drew our attention to a 1943 report: *Our Towns: A Close-up*. It was written by eight women members of the Hygiene Committee of the Women's Group on Public Welfare, who tried to explain the living conditions and family lives of children from the East End and elsewhere who had been evacuated to better-off homes. Amongst those children was Bob Holman as a young boy. Their report acted as a wake-up call for politicians and the public, contributing to greater understanding of poverty and the development of post-war social policies.

Bob challenged eight named women to undertake a similar task today. And I joined them. Because – as Julia Unwin from the Joseph Rowntree Foundation put it in her Foreword to the report – I wanted to "illuminate, and humanise, the dry accounts of trend data". And I wanted to help convey the message that attitudes to people in poverty are the biggest obstacles to positive change.

Of course, we also wanted to convey in the report the harsh impact of austerity on the lives of those who were already struggling, and several of the stories do that. One describes Alice's situation.

Alice lives with her two children aged five and eight in a three-bedroom council house. She has no formal qualifications and has difficulty reading and writing. She would like to work with children. She says she was just about coping before but is now increasingly in debt and stressed. She feels harassed by Jobcentre Plus to show she is actively seeking work. But she is also liable for the 'bedroom tax' because the children have a bedroom each. And she also now has to pay some council tax which she did not have to pay before the recent changes.

The 'bedroom tax' is a well-known reform, which means that tenants in social housing considered to have rooms additional to their needs find their housing benefit cut. But there has been less publicity about the changes to council tax benefit. The Government devolved this to local authorities, whilst simultaneously cutting the amount (and protecting pensioners and some others from cuts). So working-age people on benefit have been hit by the equivalent of the poll tax in many areas. But unlike the poll tax, no compensation whatsoever has been given in benefit levels. This should be denounced as the scandal that it is. But unlike the poll tax, this is a local issue and its impact differs from area to area, making it harder to campaign against.

A fair hearing

We also wanted to show, however, that this is not only about Coalition government policies. The first story above, about Sally and Chris, demonstrates the all-too-common experience of people in poverty, that they are not respected by public officials. Until the appeal tribunal – at which they said they at last got a fair hearing – Sally and Chris felt their side of the story was not believed.

And Jenny's story above shows this is not just about public officials. It was the bank in her case that showed not the slightest understanding of her life and situation. Other stories in the report profile private sector organisations that profit from the difficulties faced by people in poverty. Alice herself buys most of her household goods from a well-known private company, paying weekly so that she is effectively leasing it at extortionate prices: a (better quality) washing machine from a high street supplier would be less than half the price. She has to take the bus to town each week to pay off her debt – and the staff are aware of the children's birthdays, so constantly tempt her to spend more.

You could dismiss these stories as anecdotal, and in a sense they are. But they were gathered together by a group of women who, as Julia Unwin says, between us "bring decades of experience and commitment". We know these people and many others who are struggling to make ends meet, and doing so against the odds – with great resilience and endurance.

We got together to write the report with a sense of urgency. The infrastructure of welfare state support is under attack; social security is deemed to be too costly; and the lack of knowledge and understanding of the daily struggles many families face means that bridging the gap in an increasingly unequal society is becoming harder.

Our Towns, the 1943 report, reminds us that radical achievements are possible even in austere times. We hope these stories will prompt readers to ask whether this is the kind of society we really want to be. We hope that, alongside statistics and academic reports, they will act as a wake-up call to help inspire action, including and involving people living in poverty themselves in shaping proposals for change.

The eight women challenged by Bob Holman were Tricia Zipfel (community development and social policy worker), Jo Tunnard (founding director of a family rights organisation), Josephine Feeney (children's writer), Audrey Flannagan (manager of a food bank), Loretta Gaffney (Citizens Advice Bureau worker), Karen Postle (social worker), Frances O'Grady (General Secretary, TUC) and Sally Young (chief executive of a voluntary sector organisation). Fran Bennett wrote this article in a personal capacity.

5 May 2015

⇨ The above information is reprinted with kind permission from Society Central. Please visit www.societycentral.ac.uk for further information.

⇨ To read the full report, please visit http://www.ryantunnardbrown. com/wp-content/ uploads/2015/03/FINAL-Our-Lives-18-March-2015-JT-TZ-with-foreword-20-march1.pdf

Poverty among young people in the UK

A household is in poverty if its income after tax and housing costs is less than 60% of the typical (median) household income. It therefore identifies poverty as those with an income considerably below what is typical in society. A single adult with a disposable income of less than £130 per week in 2012/13 would be in poverty.

Of the 9.0 million young people aged 14–24 living in the UK, approximately 2.7 million, or 30%, are living in poverty. This includes 1.9 million young people with an income considerably below the poverty threshold (below 50% of median income). A further 740,000 young people had incomes just above the poverty threshold (above the 60% of median income but below 70%).

"Young people not living with their parents have a much higher poverty rate at 43% than those who do at 25%"

13% of young people live in families that are unable to keep their accommodation warm enough. Among children aged 14 and over, 8% do not have local access to outdoor space in which to play and 9% lack leisure equipment because of cost.

At 30%, the poverty rate among young people is higher than any other age group. A decade earlier the children aged under 14 were more likely to be in poverty than young people, but this is no longer true. The poverty rate among 20–24-year-olds grew by six percentage points in the last decade, more than any other age group.

Poverty among young people is highest in London at 38%, but the proportion of young adults in London claiming an out-of-work benefit is lower than much of the

North of England. Estimates of poverty at the local area suggest that it is highest in the Welsh Valleys, cities across England and some coastal towns.

380,000 young people in poverty have a long-standing illness or disability. Most young people in poverty are White-British (1.9 million), but the poverty rate for non-White British young people is almost double the rate for White British young people.

Of the 9.0 million people aged 14–24, 6.4 million live with their parents and 2.6 million do not. Just under half of all young people living with their parents (3.1 million) are classified as 'dependent children' (i.e. they were aged under 16, or aged 16–19, living with their parents and in full-time education).

Young people not living with their parents have a much higher poverty rate at 43% than those who do at 25%. But this gap is linked to tenure: young people not living with their parents are more likely to rent, and renters have a higher poverty rate.

Just under 1.1 million young people in poverty live in private rented accommodation, compared to 960,000 in social rented and 680,000 in owner-occupied. The poverty rate for young people in owner-occupied housing is at 15% compared to close to 50% for renters.

More than half of 19- to 24-year-olds with children are in poverty. But this only amounts to 370,000 young people, compared to 2.3 million in poverty without children. Young people with children are rarely teenagers and are much more likely to be in their mid-20s.

Some 3.1 million young people in poverty are classified as 'dependent children' (they are under 16, or up to 19, living with their parents and in full-time education). They are more likely to be in poverty if none of their parents are in work but over two thirds of those in poverty have a working parent. Of the 5.9 million young people in poverty that are classified as 'working-age adults' (aged 19 and over, or 16 and not in full-time education): 540,000 are working, 420,000 are unemployed, 380,000 are inactive and 440,000 are students.

"Poverty among young people is higher than any other age group, a decade ago this was not the case"

There are more 19- and 20-year-olds in poverty than young people of other ages. If full-time students who do not live with their parents were excluded this peak would disappear. But even excluding students the poverty rate for people in their early 20s is still five percentage points higher than for those in their late 20s.

Poverty among young people is higher than any other age group, a decade earlier this was not the case. Whilst the poverty rate for children under 14 and for pensioners fell, the poverty rate for young people increased. Part of the reason that poverty among young people is higher is that they are more likely to live in private rented accommodation and spend a greater share of their income on housing costs.

But the age group 14 to 24 is diverse. The vast majority of 14-year-olds live with their parents and are in full-time education, whilst the opposite is true for 24-year-olds; in fact, many of them will be parents themselves. The poverty rate for young people is high across the age group but their circumstances will be very different and efforts to tackle poverty need to reflect this.

13 April 2015

⇨ The above information is reprinted with kind permission from the New Policy Institute. Please visit www.npi.org.uk for further information.

"Truly dreadful" poverty rise must prompt Government action

Responding to official statistics showing 200,000 more children are now living in poverty, Matthew Reed, Chief Executive of The Children's Society, said:

"These figures are truly dreadful. The Government was repeatedly warned of the likely consequences of reducing support for the poorest people in the country and now we can see the results. Austerity has bitten hard, with an additional 200,000 children living below the poverty line. More children face missing out on hot meals, sleeping in cold bedrooms and being bullied at school. In the longer term, too many young people risk being denied a fair start and left behind, with life-changing consequences.

"The Government promotes getting families back to work as the best way of tackling child poverty, but the reality is that two thirds of children in poverty now live in working families. The four-year freeze to tax credits already in the pipeline will only make things worse. It is crucial that the Government recognises the importance of income to make sure that when parents move into work they move out of poverty.

"The situation is made even more stark by the economic uncertainty that the country faces after last Thursday's referendum result. Children did not have a role in that decision and their interests must be safeguarded first and foremost when deciding what happens next.

"The publication of these figures must prompt urgent action to protect the wellbeing of children. Whoever ends up leading the Government must rule out further welfare cuts in another emergency budget that would punish the poorest families and inevitably drag more children into poverty."

Headline stats

⇨ 3.9 million children now living in poverty after housing costs

⇨ 29% of children now living in poverty

⇨ Rise of 200,000 children living in families below 50% of median income meaning that more children are living in even deeper poverty

⇨ 66% of children in poverty have at least one parent in work, up from 62% last year.

Notes to Editor

⇨ The *Households below average income* (HBAI) statistics for 2014/15, published by the Department for Work and Pensions on 28 June 2016, are available here: https://www.gov.uk/government/statistics/households-below-average-income-199495-to-201415

⇨ The Children's Society is a national charity that runs local services, helping children and young people when they are at their most vulnerable, and have nowhere left to turn. We also campaign for changes to laws affecting children and young people, to stop the mistakes of the past being repeated in the future. Our supporters around the country fund our services and join our campaigns to show children and young people they are on their side.

28 June 2016

⇨ The above information is reprinted with kind permission from The Children's Society. Please visit www.childrenssociety.org.uk for further information.

Vulnerable young people intimidated by banks

Six out of ten (59 per cent) vulnerable young people will not go into a bank for financial information or advice, saying they find them intimidating and unhelpful, according to a report published today by Action for Children.

The charity surveyed 163 vulnerable young people, such as care leavers or young parents, about the challenges of managing money and what would help them manage money better for its report, *Getting a fair deal?*.

Young people spoke of how significant life events were when they needed to learn about money matters. Nearly three-quarters (72 per cent) of young people said it was when they leave home and 59 per cent when they have children.

Kate Mulley, Director of Policy and Campaigns, said: "Managing money is an essential life skill. Vulnerable young people are over-represented in the 12 per cent of 16- to 24-year-olds who do not have a bank account. Institutions like banks are an obvious choice for most people to get financial advice, so they need to do much more to persuade young people to drop in."

Action for Children is calling on banks and building societies to:

⇨ Design products young people can use and trust.

⇨ Use everyday language.

⇨ Train staff to understand vulnerable young people.

⇨ Tell young people where they can get extra help.

Kate Mulley added: "For young people who have had turbulent childhoods or have gone through the care system, they may have missed years of school or not had the family environment to learn basic skills from budgeting to paying bills.

"Most people worry about money. However, vulnerable young people do not have the luxury of making mistakes to learn from. One in four have told us they already struggle to pay for the bare essentials like food, so one unpaid bill or missed rent payment can mean homelessness or feeling cornered to go to high-interest lenders, making an already difficult situation insurmountable.

"For young people who have had turbulent childhoods or have gone through the care system, they may have missed years of school or not had the family environment to learn basic skills from budgeting to paying bills"

"If we help young people to take control of their finances, they will have a greater chance of finding and keeping a job and of creating a stable and happy life, making them an asset to society."

The *Getting a fair deal?* report also shows:

⇨ 67 per cent of vulnerable young people have never had financial education at school.

⇨ 74 per cent want to learn budgeting skills.

⇨ 51 per cent want to know how to manage their bills.

⇨ 19 per cent wanted to understand how banks work and what they can offer.

14 July 2015

⇨ The above information is reprinted with kind permission from Action for Children. Please visit www.actionforchildren.org.uk for further information.

RENT

FOOD

TRANSPORT / CLOTHES

ENTERTAINMENT

What is child poverty?

A family with two adults and two children under 15 needs to have £375 a week, after paying for housing, to be above the poverty line. How do you think that compares to what your family has?

£13 a day – the reality of living in poverty

Many families living on a low income have only about £13 per day per person.

This needs to cover:

⇨ all of their day-to-day expenditure, including necessities such as food and transport

⇨ occasional items such as new shoes and clothes, school trips and activities for children, and replacing broken household items such as washing machines and kitchen equipment

⇨ all household bills such as electricity, gas and water, telephone bills and TV licences.

How does living in poverty compare with the average UK family?

In 2013, average weekly spending for:

⇨ couple families with children was £664, which is equivalent to £175 per person

⇨ a couple family with an income in the lowest 20 per cent spent just £339, equivalent to £96 per person.

That's less than half what the average family spends.

There are big differences in crucial items of spending, such as health and transport:

⇨ The poorest fifth of couple families spent about £18 per week on clothing in 2013, compared to an average of £31 for all couple families.

⇨ There were even bigger differences in spending on transport, where the poorest families spent £29 per week, compared to £92 on average for all families.

What effects can child poverty have?

Living in a poor family can reduce children's expectations of their own lives and lead to a cycle where poverty is repeated from generation to generation.

As adults they are more likely to suffer ill-health, be unemployed or homeless, and become involved in offending, drug and alcohol abuse, and abusive relationships.

In tackling poverty it is crucial to break the cycle. Education is a key element of this, as are initiatives which involve people in developing their skills and finding their own solutions to the problems in their community.

How does Barnardo's help?

Barnardo's works across the UK to transform the lives of vulnerable children.

Read stories and case studies of how we have helped children and families living in poverty on the Barnardo's website.

Find out more about Barnardo's child poverty research and publications or search Barnardo's full publications database.

Child poverty statistics and facts

There are currently 3.7 million children living in poverty in the UK. That's over a quarter of all children. 1.7 million of these children are living in severe poverty. In the UK 63% of children living in poverty are in a family where someone works.

These child poverty statistics and facts will help to give you an idea of the scale of child poverty in the UK and the effect it can have on:

⇨ a child's education

⇨ a child's health

⇨ the day-to-day lives of families.

Does child poverty affect children's health?

⇨ Three-year-olds in households with incomes below about £10,000 are 2.5 times more likely to suffer chronic illness than children in households with incomes above £52,000.

⇨ Infant mortality is 10% higher for infants in the lower social group than the average.

Does poverty affect a child's education?

⇨ Only 48 per cent of five-year-olds entitled to free school meals have a good level of development at the end of their reception year, compared to 65 per cent of all other pupils.

⇨ Less than half of pupils entitled to free school meals (just 34 per cent) achieve five GCSEs at C or above, including English and Maths, this compares to 61 per cent of pupils who are not eligible.

How much money do families living in poverty have?

⇨ Families living in poverty can have as little as £13 per day per person to buy everything they need such as food, heating, toys, clothes, electricity and transport.

How does poverty affect families?

⇨ Poverty impacts on what families can spend, one in ten of the poorest families can't afford to send their children on school trips, compared to one in 100 of the richest families; 58 per cent of the poorest families would like to go on holiday once a year but cannot, only five per cent of the richest families cannot afford this luxury.

"The Government has a statutory requirement, enshrined in the Child Poverty Act 2010, to end child poverty by 2020. However, it is predicated that by 2020/21 another one million children will be pushed into poverty as a result of the Coalition Government's policies."

⇨ The above information is reprinted with kind permission from Barnardo's. Please visit www.barnardos.org.uk for further information.

© Barnardo's 2016

Poor Mental Health – The links between child poverty and mental health problems

An extract from the report by The Children's Society.

Definitions of mental health and poverty

Mental health

Throughout the report, the term 'mental health problems' is used to describe different conditions children and teenagers can experience. This includes mild, moderate to severe and ensuing conditions, ranging from anxiety or depression through to bipolar disorder, schizophrenia and eating disorders. We recognise a range of terms exist to describe these conditions and illnesses, but for consistency and clarity we are using the term 'mental health problems' throughout this report.

Wellbeing

The Children's Society has been studying children's subjective wellbeing since 2005. The Good Childhood Inquiry, launched in 2006, was the first independent national inquiry into childhood that sought to better understand modern childhood from the perspective of children themselves.

Since 2012 we have produced annual reports reviewing children's subjective wellbeing and have analysed the impact of a range of factors affecting the way children feel about their lives.

Subjective wellbeing is about children's own assessment of how their lives are going. Are children satisfied with their relationships with the significant people in their lives? Are they satisfied with the environments that they inhabit and how they spend their time? Are they satisfied with how they see themselves? Which aspects of their lives do they rate highly, and which do they rate poorly? How are their lives going at present, and how do they feel about the way things are heading? Subjective wellbeing is based on two elements:

⇨ life satisfaction

⇨ experience of positive and negative emotions at a particular point in time.

Psychological wellbeing is concerned with children's sense of meaning, purpose and engagement. Our research also found that children's subjective wellbeing has a moderate association with measures of mental health problems – suggesting that there is a link between the two things, but that they are nevertheless distinct

Child poverty

Townsend, in his 1979 book *Poverty in the United Kingdom*, defined this as lacking "the resources to obtain the types of diets, participate in the activities, and have the living conditions and amenities that are customary... in the societies to which they belong". Such resources may include money in itself, but they may also include other forms of material resources – such as access to healthcare, a decent home and a high-quality free education. Children are said to live in relative income poverty if they live in households with income below 60% of the household median. This relative child poverty measure recognises that it is not enough that children's basic needs are met, but they also have the resources necessary for them to participate in the same activities as their peers.

Evidence of the links between poverty and children's emotional wellbeing and mental health

Understanding society analysis

This section outlines our analysis of Understanding Society's 2015 data release, a longitudinal data set that covers areas such as income, housing, health and wellbeing. We have focused on 16- to 19-year-olds living in poverty as these are the most relevant for this research. Therefore, whilst it is not a comprehensive assessment of all children, it offers an indication as to the impact of growing up in poverty on the emotional wellbeing of young people.

The impact of poverty on the wellbeing of 16- to 19-year-olds

Our analysis of the Understanding Society survey has shown that there is an association between children aged between 16 and 19 living in

poverty and their emotional wellbeing. For instance, the way that children and young people view themselves and the way that they feel about their future prospects both have significant correlations with living in poverty.

Children and young people growing up in poverty feel distinctly less optimistic about the future than their more affluent peers. This in turn has a knock-on detrimental effect on their aspirations and the potential that they believe the future holds for them.

Another correlation between poverty and emotional wellbeing is how useful children in poverty feel, with almost a quarter (22%) saying that they didn't feel useful compared to one in six children from more affluent backgrounds.

This combination of lack of optimism and self-worth suggests a negative association between growing up in poverty for children and young people's emotional wellbeing. This insight is further reinforced by the number of children and young people growing up in poverty reporting that they "feel a failure", with the evidence gathered from our analysis showing that they are considerably more likely to report this than their more affluent peers.

Poverty, relationships with family and friends, and children's mental health

There is evidence to suggest that being born into poverty can increase the risk of mental health problems in children and young people, which in turn can have long-term consequences for their educational outcomes and social relationships. In a recent report the Children and Young People's Mental Health Coalition highlighted that "being born into poverty puts children at greater risk of mental health problems and, for many, this will lead to negative consequences through their lives, affecting educational attainment and social relationships, and can be cumulative".

The negative consequences of living in poverty were well illustrated in our recent work on the Children's Commission on Poverty (CCP), which showed that children are acutely aware that their parents struggle with

the cost of school. Where children were struggling with school costs, in many cases this led to embarrassment and bullying. Nearly two-thirds (63%) of children in families who are "not well-off at all" said they had been embarrassed because they couldn't afford the cost of school, such as a school trip or a new item of uniform.

This highlights the stigma which may be associated with growing up in poverty. Young people told us that they felt marginalised or misunderstood as a result of their teachers and peers not appreciating the realities of living in poverty. Being able to interact with their peer group is important for children and young people as they grow up, and this suggests that growing up in poverty makes it harder to do so.

Stigma and poverty

Stigma from those around them, be that their friends, peers more broadly, or society as a whole, can have an impact on the emotional wellbeing of children and young people growing up in poverty. It may contribute to the higher likelihood of "feeling a failure" and a lack of optimism for the future, as described previously. Analysis by the Health and Social Care Information Centre has found that one in six 15-year-olds in the UK who come from deprived areas reported having low life satisfaction, compared with around one in ten of those living in the least deprived areas. The young people involved in the CCP echoed this. One young person who contributed to the Commission told us:

"We are still judged on it now sometimes, some people say 'oh it's a council house kid'…it makes me feel quite angry, maybe their family hasn't got enough to buy them clothes straight away, maybe they can't afford the water bill."

Furthermore, research by Mind has shown that perceived stigma leads to loneliness, depression and loss of confidence, and that the fear of this type of discrimination can be as damaging as actual discrimination. This can have a distinctly negative effect on young people's view of the world, and their place in it, which has an inhibiting impact on their ability

to achieve their full potential, both at school and also as they grow up and move into employment.

Comparing children and young people in poverty with those from more affluent backgrounds

Over the last 25 years research has shown that growing up in poverty has a detrimental effect on the mental health and wellbeing of children and young people. There is evidence to suggest that children and young people who live in poverty have a higher chance of experiencing mental health problems and lower subjective wellbeing both as children, and as adults.

Research published by the Department of Health in 1999 outlined that children in the poorest households are "three times more likely to have a mental illness than children in the best-off households". This is made all the more concerning when evidence shows the impact of persistent and deep poverty on the mental health of children and young people.

Original analysis of the National Child Development Study data between 1958 and 2008 by the Centre for Longitudinal Studies has shown that children from the lowest income families are four times more likely (16%) to display psychological problems than children from the richest families (4%). This is further reinforced by evidence that shows children in poverty "have more mental health problems than non-poor children, whether we consider internalising problems like depression or externalising problems like antisocial behaviour".

This raises the possibility that addressing child poverty could also have a positive impact on improving children's mental health outcomes.

March 2016

⇨ The above information is reprinted with kind permission from The Children's Society. Please visit www.childrenssociety.org for further information.

Poverty and children's personal and social relationships

In the ongoing debate about how to measure and address poverty in the UK, it is crucial to understand how living with low income affects children. While the evidence base is fairly strong in areas like education and health, poverty's role in shaping relationships is less well understood. This research explored associations between poverty and children's relationships, using Millennium Cohort Study data.

Key points

Overall, 11-year-olds reported positive relationships with their peers, though one in six described being bullied on a weekly basis. Likewise, they presented a positive picture of family relationships, though more than one in five reported that siblings hurt or picked on them "most days".

Poverty, especially persistent poverty, was associated with more problematic interaction with peers, on several measures. However, children with experience of poverty were just as likely to be happy with their friends, and typically spent more time with them outside school.

Poverty was also associated with aspects of parent-child relationships. Those from less-well-off families reported slightly lower levels of communication and closeness and higher levels of conflict. However, children from low-income homes were just as likely as their peers to be happy with their families.

After taking into account other factors, including child behaviour, maternal mental health and parental engagement, most links between poverty and children's

> ### Poverty and peer relationships
> Compared with children with no experience of poverty, those persistently experiencing poverty were:
>
> ⇨ more likely to fight with or bully others (16.4 per cent of those in persistent poverty versus 3.8 per cent of those never in poverty);
>
> ⇨ more likely to be bullied most days (11.6 per cent versus 4.6 per cent);
>
> ⇨ more likely to play alone (35.7 per cent versus 26.2 per cent).
>
> ⇨ less likely to have a good friend (83.9 per cent versus 91.4 per cent);
>
> ⇨ less likely to talk to friends about their worries (34.1 per cent versus 42.5 per cent).

relationships were no longer statistically significant. However, persistent poverty was still associated with greater interaction with friends outside school, and more frequent fights with, or bullying of, peers. In addition, once other factors were taken into account, persistent poverty was associated with higher levels of happiness with families.

Poverty's effects on children's relationships appeared to be mostly indirect. A broad range of risk factors were more likely to affect those from low-income homes, including maternal mental health problems, low levels of parental education, lower cognitive ability and special educational needs.

The research by Jen Gibb, Katie Rix and Emma Wallace (National Children's Bureau) and Emla Fitzsimons and Tarek Mostafa (Centre for Longitudinal Studies).

March 2016

⇨ The above information is from *Poverty and children's personal and social relationships* by Jen Gibb, Katie Rix, Emma Wallace, Emla Fitzsimons and Tarek Mostafa, published in 2016 by the Joseph Rowntree Foundation. Reproduced by permission of the Joseph Rowntree Foundation.

Research reveals impact of the school holidays on struggling families

More than six out of ten parents with household incomes of less than £25,000 are struggling to feed their children outside of term time according to crucial new research by Northumbria University.

For households with incomes of less than £15,000, that figure rose to 73% of parents who said they weren't always able to afford to buy food outside of term time.

The findings particularly affect those families receiving a free school meal, which ensures that children are guaranteed at least one wholesome meal a day.

Research on school holiday hunger by 'Healthy Living' at Northumbria University has fed into a Kellogg's report – *Isolation and Hunger: the impact of the school holidays on struggling families* – which was delivered to MPs on Friday (17 July).

Professor Greta Defeyter, Director of Healthy Living at Northumbria University, led the research, which was commissioned by Kellogg's.

It revealed 71% of parents found it harder to make ends meet during the summer holidays compared with term-time, while 63% of parents find themselves without enough money for food during the summer. A staggering 93% of low-income parents skip at least one meal a day to make sure their children are fed.

More than 65% of parents on low household incomes say they often feel isolated in the school holidays due to being unable to afford to feed their families, or go out and entertain their children.

A pilot of 12 Kellogg's breakfast clubs delivered over the summer holiday period of 2014, revealed that clubs were positively received by children, staff and parents and all groups were keen to see the provision made available during future school holidays.

Kellogg's has now developed a holiday breakfast club programme based on these findings and has committed funding to the Mayor's Fund for London to help run ten clubs in the capital until August 2016.

Child poverty is set to become more commonly felt across the country, and particularly in the North East, as the impact of recent budget cuts come into effect, says Professor Defeyter. More than 37% of children are in poverty in the Newcastle Central constituency and in the ward of Elswick this increases to 47.5%

Professor Defeyter said: "There has been a 500,000-strong rise in the number of children in poverty, and many families have reacted by serving food laden with salt, fat and sugar because it is perceived as more filling food for the money.

"We know that food poverty becomes more acute during school holidays. The question is, why help? Well, it's a basic human right to have access to food for a healthy diet, and we know there's a clear link between food and academic attainment – particularly in areas of poverty and among primary-age children.

"We are doing something about it in term time, but what about during the holidays?"

To help families in need, Kellogg's is partnering with FareShare, which provides food to over 2,000 charities and community projects including holiday breakfast clubs.

Kellogg's director Paul Wheeler said: "This summer there'll be tens of thousands of parents going without meals so they can feed their kids.

"We are trying to help these parents by funding free holiday breakfast clubs across the UK. Those already open have proven to be a great success. That's why we've invited politicians from all political parties to visit the clubs this summer to draw attention to this issue and demonstrate that there is help available."

Northumbria's research in the field of Psychology, which includes its work on breakfast clubs, was judged to have outstanding reach and significance for its impact on society in the 2014 Research Excellence Framework exercise, which assesses the quality of research in UK universities.

20 July 2015

⇨ The above information is reprinted with kind permission from the University of Northumbria at Newcastle.

Pensioners 'eating less' to make ends meet, claims study

By Jody Harrison

Pensioners are being forced to make major sacrifices to their lifestyles as their finances come under increasing pressure, new research has found.

A study of over-60s living in the UK found that almost one in three say that they struggle to make ends meet and have had to change they way they live in the face of rising costs for heating, food and luxuries.

According to the study by property experts Homewise, one in three over-60s said that cutbacks have lead to them borrowing money from friends and family and resorting to selling possessions because they do not have enough cash to live off.

And one in ten have turned down the heating to save money and even started eating less in a bid to stave off poverty.

The research underlines the growing financial pressures on people in the run up to retirement and highlights the struggle for millions despite the rise in average pensioner incomes.

Westminster figures show average pensioner household incomes after tax and housing costs are around £297 a week, while household incomes have increased by around 19 per cent over the past decade.

But the Homewise study found that around 600,000 over-60s, the equivalent of 7 per cent of the UK population, have less than £50 a week in spare cash while millions of others have to make major sacrifices.

Mark Neal, Managing Director at Homewise, said: "The rise in average pensioner incomes is very welcome, but it does not tell the whole story and the sacrifices that many have to make in order to get by.

"Far too many people in retirement are stuck in debt, living in unsuitable housing and having to scrimp and save."

Meanwhile, a separate study has suggested that middle-aged and elderly people can boost their mental wellbeing by volunteering,

Previous research has linked volunteering to mental wellbeing, but it is the first time that researchers have examined whether it is beneficial to different age groups.

The new study, published in the journal *BMJ Open*, examined data from 5,000 households across the UK. Questions on volunteering were asked on numerous occasions between 1996 and 2008.

Participants were also asked about their general health and wellbeing.

The authors, from the universities of Southampton and Birmingham, found that, when not considering age, those who engaged in volunteering regularly appeared to experience higher levels of mental wellbeing than those who never volunteered.

But when they looked into volunteering across different age groups, they discovered the association between volunteering and wellbeing only became apparent above the age of 40 years and continuing up to old age.

"The association between volunteering and mental wellbeing varies at different points in the life course," the authors wrote.

"These findings argue for more efforts to involve middle-aged people to older people in volunteering-related activities.

"Volunteering action might provide those groups with greater opportunities for beneficial activities and social contacts, which in turn may have protective effects on health status."

9 August 2016

⇨ The above information is reprinted with kind permission from *Herald Scotland*. Please visit www.heraldscotland.com for further information.

Food poverty

Food poverty means that an individual or household isn't able to obtain healthy, nutritious food, or can't access the food they would like to eat. Despite increasing choice and affordability of food in the UK, many people eat what they can afford, not what they want.

This often results in people eating poor diets, which can lead to heart disease, obesity, diabetes and cancer, as well as inadequate levels of many vitamins and minerals. Obesity is now as much a sign of poverty in the rich countries, as hunger is in poor countries.

Food poverty and economic poverty are linked. Rent, tax and debts are fixed costs; food is the 'flexible' budget item, and families and individuals pay the price.

Poor children suffer from lower nutrient intake, bad dietary patterns, hunger, low fruit and vegetable consumption and problems accessing food in school holidays.

A 2014 report by Oxfam UK, The Trussell Trust and Church Action

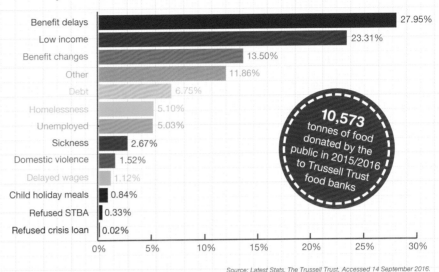

Primary reasons for referral to Trussell Trust food banks, 2015–2016

Reason	Percentage
Benefit delays	27.95%
Low income	23.31%
Benefit changes	13.50%
Other	11.86%
Debt	6.75%
Homelessness	5.10%
Unemployed	5.03%
Sickness	2.67%
Domestic violence	1.52%
Delayed wages	1.12%
Child holiday meals	0.84%
Refused STBA	0.33%
Refused crisis loan	0.02%

10,573 tonnes of food donated by the public in 2015/2016 to Trussell Trust food banks

Source: Latest Stats, The Trussell Trust, Accessed 14 September 2016.

on Poverty revealed that over 20 million meals were provided in 2013 to people in the UK who could not afford to feed themselves – a 54% increase on the previous 12 months.

Claims and counter-claims abound over the reasons for increasing food poverty levels in the UK, but whatever the cause, it's shocking that in a wealthy society, where

tonnes of perfectly good food is thrown away on a daily basis, people are going to bed hungry at night. Things need to change.

The Government has a responsibility to identify and address the structural inequalities in household income and access to food that contribute to food poverty. Minimum wage and benefit levels should be sufficient to ensure that all households have a living income, not merely a survival income. And food retailers should proactively seek to ensure that the healthiest foods are affordable and accessible to all.

In 2013 the Food Ethics Council and the University of Warwick undertook a research project for the Department of Food, Environment and Rural Affairs to arrive at a better understanding of the 'food aid' landscape in the UK and the 'at risk' individuals who access such provision, as well as the means and drivers for seeking access.

⇨ The above information is reprinted with kind permission from the Food Ethics Council. Please visit www. foodethicscouncil.org for further information.

© Food Ethics Council 2016

Latest food bank figures top 900,000: life has got worse not better...

... for poorest in 2013/14, and this is just the tip of the iceberg.

⇨ 913,138 people received three days' emergency food from Trussell Trust food banks in 2013–14 compared to 346,992 in 2012–13

⇨ Figures are "tip of the iceberg" of UK food poverty says Trussell Trust Chairman

⇨ 83% of food banks report 'sanctioning' is causing rising numbers to turn to them

⇨ Food bank figures trigger biggest ever faith leader intervention on UK food poverty in modern times.

Over 900,000 adults and children have received three days' emergency food and support from Trussell Trust food banks in the last 12 months, a shocking 163 per cent rise on numbers helped in the previous financial year. Despite signs of economic recovery, the poorest have seen incomes squeezed even more than last year reports The Trussell Trust, the UK's largest food bank network. More people are being referred to Trussell Trust food banks than ever before.

Static incomes, rising living costs, low pay, underemployment and problems with welfare, especially sanctioning, are significant drivers of the increased demand. 83 per cent of Trussell Trust food banks surveyed recently reported that benefits sanctions, which have become increasingly harsh, have caused more people to be referred to them for emergency food. Half of referrals to food banks in 2013–14 were a result of benefit delays or changes.

The Trussell Trust's Chairman, Chris Mould, says:

"That 900,000 people have received three days' food from a food bank, close to triple the numbers helped last year, is shocking in 21st-century Britain. But perhaps most worrying of all, this figure is just the tip of the iceberg of UK food poverty, it doesn't include those helped by other emergency food providers, those living in towns where there is no food bank, people who are too ashamed to seek help or the large number of people who are only just coping by eating less and buying cheap food.

"In the last year we've seen things get worse, rather than better, for many people on low incomes. It's been extremely tough for a lot of people, with parents not eating properly in order to feed their children and more people than ever experiencing seemingly unfair and harsh benefits sanctions.

"Unless there is determined policy action to ensure that the benefits of national economic recovery reach people on low incomes we won't see life get better for the poorest anytime soon.

"A more thoughtful approach to the administration of the benefits regime and sanctions in particular, increasing the minimum wage, introducing the living wage and looking at other measures such as social tariffs for essentials like energy would help to address the problem of UK hunger."

Whilst there has been a 163 per cent increase in food bank use, there has only been a 45 per cent increase in the number of new Trussell Trust food banks opening in the last year. The rate of new food banks opening has reduced from three a week in 2012–13 to two a week in 2013–14. The Trussell Trust has launched over 400 food banks across the UK to date.

Food banks that have been open for three years or more have seen an average increase of 51 per cent in numbers helped in 2013–14 compared to 2012–13, showing that well-established food banks are experiencing significant uplift in demand.

The Trussell Trust's figures further reinforce evidence from the recent government-commissioned DEFRA report that increased food bank use is not a question of supply, but of meeting a real and growing need.

Increasingly, Trussell Trust food banks are partnering with other agencies to provide additional services such as welfare advice, budgeting help and debt support at the food bank, helping people to break out of crisis. They are also providing essentials like washing powder, nappies and hygiene products to families who are at breaking point.

New letter marks biggest ever faith intervention on food poverty in modern times:

Today a letter co-signed by 36 Anglican Bishops and over 600 church leaders from all major denominations will call for urgent government action to be taken on UK food poverty.

The letter, initiated by End Hunger Fast, will be delivered to the constituency offices of each of the three main party leaders by three church leaders who have been fasting for 40 days in solidarity with people facing hunger in the UK. This will mark the biggest ever faith leader intervention on UK food poverty in modern times.

There will also be a public vigil led by End Hunger Fast opposite Parliament at Old Palace Yard at 6pm. At the vigil, Rabbi Laura Janner-Klausner, Senior Rabbi at Movement for Reform Judaism, will for the first time publicly express the cross-communal support of the Jewish community for action against UK food poverty.

Academics are also expected to add their voice to the growing groundswell of public concern at the growth of UK hunger.

Chris Mould says: "We are encouraged that there is a growing public concern over the problem of UK hunger. Faith leaders, academics, charities and MPs are all standing up to say that hunger is not acceptable in Britain, and that is what gives us hope for change."

16 April 2014

⇨ Information from Trussell Trust. Please visit www.trusselltrust. org for further information.

Why one of the wealthiest countries in the world is failing to feed its people

An article from The Conversation.

THE CONVERSATION

By Megan Blake, Director of the MA Food Security and Food Justice, University of Sheffield

On 8 May 2015 I awoke to discover that not only were we not looking forward to a new Coalition Government in the UK, but that the overall collapse of the Liberal Democrats and the Labour Party had given the Conservative Government a mandate. At an individual level I'm likely to see some benefits from the strong neo-liberalism that underpins this Government's ideology, but I'm concerned about a further deepening of the division between those who have and those who have not.

This will mean the continued exponential growth in the numbers of people requiring emergency food assistance and increased numbers of children and elderly with inadequate food supply. This will also translate into higher rates of obesity, diet-related illness and malnutrition.

The most vulnerable

In the United Kingdom there are nearly five million people today living as food insecure. Wendy Wills, an expert in food and public health, defines this as those who are unable to acquire or consume an adequate quality or sufficient quantity of food made available in socially acceptable ways, or who have the (regular) uncertainty that they will be able to do so.

In 2014, more than 20 million meals were provided to people unable to provide for themselves. Since 2010 there has been an exponential growth in the number of households relying on emergency food aid. In 2009–10 nearly 50,000 households received three days of emergency food aid but by 2014–15 the number had increased to more than a million. Oxfam UK has estimated that: "36% of the UK population are just one heating bill or broken washing machine away from hardship".

Poor distribution

Looking at these figures one might think the UK is not a wealthy nation. But this is not the case. Credit Suisse put the UK fifth in a ranking of nations by wealth, behind the US, Japan, China and France. Based on 2010 UK Census figures, per capita wealth in the UK is about US$182,825, but this wealth is not distributed evenly across the population. While the wealthiest fifth of the population controls nearly 41% of the income, the poorest fifth have just 8%. And while rates of employment have increased over the last few years, pay growth has not kept up.

The new Government has little in its manifesto to indicate relief, instead there are promises to cut public spending by a further £55 billion by 2019 (on top of the £35 billion cut during the Coalition Government). We have already seen cuts in work programmes that support those with disabilities in their first week in office. In the firing line are Sure Start programmes and programmes for refugees and migrants while reduced funding for local authorities will mean not only cuts to programmes that support the most vulnerable but also cuts to other services providing things such as road repairs, parks and libraries.

On top of the loss of services and support programmes, cuts also translate into bodies out of employment. So this new round of austerity will reach higher up the ladder for those living in the UK because a large proportion of the costs associated with these services is the wages for those who deliver them. The Office for Budget Responsibility indicates that by 2020 there will be a further loss of a million government jobs (compared to the loss of 400,000 government jobs over the course of the last parliament). One can only conclude that income inequality will widen, a state that already has one of the highest divisions between wealthy and poor in Europe (only lower than Turkey and Portugal in 2010).

Disposable income

For those living in poverty in the UK today the amount of disposable income for the poorest fifth of households is about £156 per week. This is income after taxes and transfer payments and includes spending on clothing, getting to work, childcare, keeping warm, washing, communicating with others, paying for housing, celebrating birthdays, holidays, paying for school trips, uniforms and supplies, socialising and cooking (including not just the food but also the fuel to run the cooker, microwave and refrigerator).

For many households (not just the poorest), the most flexible item in their budget is food expenditure. Families in this position are not concerned with the environmental or social implications associated with the food that they buy, but instead concentrate on "getting fed". Because it is now less expensive to feed one's family on processed food (with higher salt, sugar and fat content) than fresh food and as the cost of food is predicted to continue to rise, we can expect to see not just increases in the numbers of people going hungry and relying on emergency food aid, but also increases in the rates of dietary-related illnesses such as obesity, diabetes and malnutrition. These health implications will, in turn, continue to place greater pressure on an already struggling NHS.

Obligations made

The Government has an obligation to ensure that the right for all human beings to be free from hunger, food insecurity and malnutrition, as specified in a UN covenant to which the UK is a signatory, is upheld. The UK is also a signatory to the UN Convention on the Rights of the Child, which specifies a duty to provide "material assistance and support programmes, particularly with regard to nutrition".

At present the rolling back of social services, the decline in real wages, increases in food costs coupled with an emphasis within the Conservative manifesto to develop food production in this country as an export (as opposed to subsidising it in order to feed the nation), suggests that this obligation is not one that is being taken seriously.

If we cannot look to our national government to uphold these rights and obligations, it seems that there is no recourse but to fill the gap from within, something the Conservatives are banking on. In their manifesto, the only mention of food justice is expressed via the following phrase:

"We have always believed that churches, faith groups and other voluntary groups play an important and long-standing role in this country's social fabric, running food banks, helping the homeless and tackling debt and addictions, such as alcoholism and gambling. In the short term it is evident that the public will need to rely on each other to support the most vulnerable, which includes the elderly and children."

Food banks and charity are not a long-term solution, nor are they an adequate solution. We know that food banks are an insecure form of support as they rely on gifts which can be withdrawn at any time. Their coverage is spatially uneven as they are more likely to be located in cities leaving the rural poor in a more precarious position. Donated food also tends to be non-perishable food, as opposed to fresh food free of E numbers, fat, salt and sugar. Food banks also do not address more structural issues that give rise to food insecurity in the first instance. The Trussel Trust, which runs many food banks, does offer some ancillary support but this still focuses on individuals, not on the wider problems.

No single department is responsible

As a country we need a better understanding of the resources available to local authorities who bear the burden of addressing the inequalities associated with food and who must deliver services to the poor.

As citizens we also need to demand that the Government meets its UN obligations to ensure the right to food and the rights of the child.

This cannot happen within existing government departments as the focus of these rights is not embedded within any one single agency. We have the Food Standards Agency, but its remit doesn't address food access. DEFRA's focus is on food production and agriculture. The Department of Health's focus is on nutrition outcomes rather than the root causes of obesity and the structure of food system in the UK. The Department for Work and Pensions similarly only considers those elements that are employment-focused.

We currently have subsidies for winter fuel, transportation and housing, but there is nothing that ensures food affordability. What is called for is a cross-cutting governmental body, with a minister for food, who ensures that policies enacted through these departments deliver access to sufficient, healthy, affordable and culturally appropriate food for all of us, not just the wealthy.

19 May 2016

⇨ The above information is reprinted with kind permission from *The Conversation*. Please visit www.theconversation.com for further information.

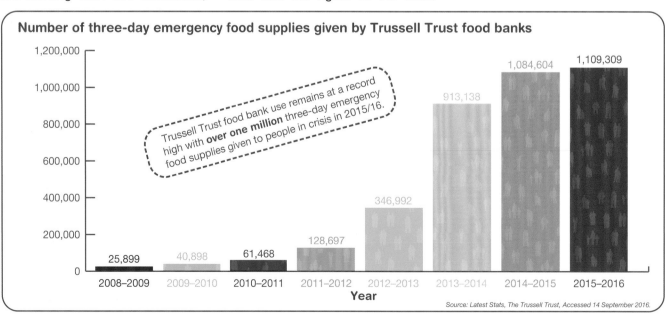

Number of three-day emergency food supplies given by Trussell Trust food banks

Trussell Trust food bank use remains at a record high with **over one million** three-day emergency food supplies given to people in crisis in 2015/16.

Year	Number
2008–2009	25,899
2009–2010	40,898
2010–2011	61,468
2011–2012	128,697
2012–2013	346,992
2013–2014	913,138
2014–2015	1,084,604
2015–2016	1,109,309

Source: Latest Stats, The Trussell Trust, Accessed 14 September 2016.

Poverty-hit Scottish pupils "stealing food"

Scottish pupils are having to steal food to avoid going hungry, according to a new survey.

More than half of teachers polled by the Education Institute of Scotland (EIS) union reported an increase in the number of pupils coming to school without food such as the 'play-piece' that has been a tradition in Scottish playgrounds.

And some 20 per cent of respondents identified an increase in the number of incidents of children asking for and even stealing food from other pupils.

In addition, the survey identified increases in the number of older children taking free school meals, an increased attendance at breakfast clubs and a rising number of parents requesting referrals to local foodbanks in order to feed their children.

On the issue of pupils' health and wellbeing, the survey found 71 per cent of teachers reporting an increase in the number of children displaying signs of mental health including anxiety, stress and low mood.

Reported instances of physical ill-health also increased, with 52 per cent of those surveyed highlighting an increase in indicators such as headaches and lethargy.

Larry Flanagan, general secretary of the EIS, said the findings were a "stark warning" of the "deep and damaging impact" of poverty and the politics of austerity on pupils.

He said: "One of the most troubling findings is evidence of increasing food poverty affecting more pupils in our schools and the worrying increase in the theft of food which highlights the desperate circumstances many children are finding themselves in.

"The fact teachers are reporting such very high increases in both mental and physical health issues in pupils is also a huge concern and highlights

the true cost of political choices that have driven more families into poverty and widened the gap between the rich and the poor."

A spokesman for local authority umbrella body COSLA said councils were deeply concerned about the impact of poverty in their communities, but warned the situation would get worse following the Scottish Government's last budget – which will see £350 million cuts to local government.

He said: "Whether through helping vulnerable older people, giving care leavers the support they need to stand on their own feet or helping young unemployed people into sustainable jobs, local government is central to the fight against poverty.

"Knowing this makes the inevitable cuts that are being forced on local services by the Scottish Government all the harder to make.

"The Scottish Government has chosen to cut funding for services that are helping the most vulnerable which, in our view, risks making poverty in Scotland even worse."

A Scottish Government spokesman said the findings were "truly

shocking" and said no child should be going to school hungry.

He added: "This government is taking many positive actions to tackle the impacts of poverty on our children from scrapping prescription charges to encouraging employers to pay the living wage.

"We are also investing £296 million over three years to protect people from UK Government's welfare cuts and austerity agenda which are increasing the numbers of children living in poverty."

The Scottish Government also highlighted its policy to provide free school meals for all P1–P3 pupils which has seen an uptake of some 80 per cent.

31 December 2015

⇨ The above information is reprinted with kind permission from *Herald Scotland*. Please visit www.heraldscotland.com for further information.

In their own words: the astonishing rise of food banks

Winesses to the all-party inquiry into food poverty graphically reveal both the causes of UK food poverty and the devastating human impact.

By Patrick Butler

The all-party parliamentary group on food poverty and hunger gathered some astonishing and often harrowing evidence from food bank clients, volunteers, public servants and the charities during its eight-month inquiry during April and November this year.

It found hunger was affecting people all over the country: in urban and rural areas, in wealthy towns and deprived neighbourhoods, with often devastating effects on lives and families.

Here's a flavour of the evidence, which cumulatively describes the reasons for both the rapid escalation of food banks, the scale of food poverty, and its human impact.

The inquiry found food banks have become an emergency response to a dramatic recent rise in food poverty, even in traditionally poor areas, Nigel Hughes, the chief executive of YMCA Wirral told the inquiry:

"This area [Wirral] has had a number of problems with deprivation for a long time. But it has never, ever reached the point as it has recently where deprivation necessitates the urgent forming of a food bank."

But it is not just poorer areas which has seen people going hungry. The social responsibility adviser to the Diocese of Oxford, Alison Webster, said:

"This is the town [in wealthy Berkshire] where one of the three food bank directors discovered a woman in the advanced stages of pregnancy and her partner living in a child's toy tent in winter, with nothing to eat, down a lane less than 200 yards from one of the churches."

Some charities were taken aback by their unexpected new role as a sticking plaster for gaps in the welfare state. Mark Goodway, director of The Matthew Tree Project in Bristol, told the inquiry:

"What we were set up to do in the first place wasn't to support people with no money at all because their benefits had been withdrawn. That wasn't what we were all about. We've been sucked in by accident. What we were about was helping people with deep-seated, long-term problems. We'd like to give the limited resource we've got to those people. But we're regularly supporting people with benefit delays for six, eight or 12 weeks, otherwise they'd have nothing."

Leeds Food Aid Network said it had historically associated food poverty with people who were homeless. But this had changed in recent years

"More recently, with the rise in living costs, including food prices, stagnant wages, a rise in insecure zero hour contracts and major changes to the welfare system, many more people, who are not necessarily in immediate danger of becoming homeless, have been experiencing rising levels of food poverty. This has stirred a significant increase in food banks provision which has emerged substantially in Leeds since the beginning of 2013."

Nuneaton food bank said it had even witnessed NHS workers forced to use the food bank because of low pay:

"Nuneaton does not have a lot of highly paid employment. Some of the employees at the hospital have had to supplement (their income) with food bank [parcels] on longer months."

Police officers suggested to the inquiry one consequence of the rise in hunger has been an increase in so-called "survival crime". Nicky Gjorven, a duty sergeant with Northumbria Police, said:

"Shoplifting has been a big issue in the last three years, particularly from 40–60-year-olds. It's now your essentials rather than your alcohol and your sweets that were stolen in the past. It used to be obvious why people were stealing – they were an alcoholic or a drug addict. But now people are taking the opportunity to steal staple goods."

Food poverty often drove people to desperate lengths. The inquiry heard an account of:

"One man in Birmingham who had made a mistake on his application for Jobseeker's Allowance. He received no money for 12 weeks. During the 12 weeks he was seen rummaging in the bins behind a chip shop. When the owner of the chip shop got fed up with him rummaging through the bins and phoned the police, the man was arrested for trespassing."

According to food bank client Alan McNickle of Salisbury:

"I have slept rough for a period of time and even served a jail sentence for thieving things, just to survive. I've robbed out of skips behind Iceland and slept under the river bridge by Tesco's. That's how bad it got."

The reported health consequences of going without food were often devastating. A primary school governor in Birkenhead said:

"[One lady] told me last week that she had been fine until she lost her job, with no support she soon found she did not have enough money to meet her commitments. Good food was sacrificed and a few weeks later she was admitted to hospital suffering from malnutrition. She had eaten impoverished food for weeks and then not eaten for five days as she had no money to buy food."

In one case the experience of extreme levels of poverty and hunger was fatal. Vince Hessey, of YMCA Wirral, told the inquiry:

"One of our clients was sanctioned. He had no money for 17 weeks. He was scavenging in a bin, the lorry came, picked him up and he was crushed to death."

Some witnesses said the standard food parcels were insufficient to help people who were so poor they could not afford to cook the food. According to the Alabare Centre in Salisbury:

"Our staff... had experienced service users being forced to hand back parts of their food parcels because they have been unable to afford the energy costs of heating the food."

A Birkenhead primary school governor told the inquiry:

"For the first time I have ever known we have had children crying at the end of the day as they did not want to go home to a cold dark home with no food. We had no option but to send them home. I have been in schools for 25 years and have never lost sleep over the plight of our children before, which I do now."

Many witnesses blamed the slow, cumbersome and punitive welfare system for pushing vulnerable people into food poverty. Rosie Rushton, a volunteer at Northampton food bank told the inquiry of:

"An ex-Army guy who had gone 11 weeks [without payment] and was living on the streets cooking on a makeshift brick-and-wood fire."

Benefit applications often got "lost in the system", as Winston Waller, of the Whitstable Society of St Vincent de Paul told the inquiry:

"[A woman] had a baby and applied for Child Benefit. After waiting four weeks, the benefit office contacted her to say they had lost the baby's birth certificate and so she had to buy another, which cost her £12. The benefits office then wrote to say they had found the original certificate, but had lost her form. She had to then apply again and was told it would introduce a further eight week delay."

Tighter sanctions, where claimants had benefits stopped for often absurdly minor or apparent unfair transgressions also drove food bank use. The inquiry heard many examples, including this, from Ely food bank, of a mother who had called the jobcentre to say she had to miss an appointment there because her child was ill. She was sanctioned anyway:

"Job Centre staff apparently told the claimant that it was more important to report on time at the Job Centre than take their baby to an emergency doctor's appointment."

The Faculty for Public Health at the Royal College of Physicians told the inquiry that recorded food bank demand was likely to be an underestimate of the true scale of hunger:

"Food bank numbers are an inadequate indicator of need, because many households only ask for emergency food help as a last resort... We view the rise of food poverty as an indication of the reversal of what was a long process of improvement in food availability and affordability since World War Two."

Some witnesses noted that demand was increasing beyond the capacity of voluntary food banks to help. The Catholic Church said in its submission that:

"Food banks were initially established to meet emergency need. This need has now developed into a chronic problem, which cannot be solved in the short-term with just three food parcels. There is a growing recognition that limited parcels are not enough."

The capacity of the voluntary food bank model – and the ability of individual food donors to keep them stocked – in the face of such demand was uncertain, according to some

witnesses. According to Malcolm Peirce, director of the Readifood charity:

"In our opinion the food model of donations is probably not sustainable long term. Supermarket customers will not give indefinitely without good cause."

But even some more substantial corporate donations were erratic, and often beyond the capacity of food banks to handle, as this astonishing piece of evidence from Don Gardner of Camborne, Pool and Redruth food bank illustrates:

"I had 9,864 Cornish pasties [offered to me] because the lorry was 17 minutes late to Morrisons. That shouldn't happen. I was offered 30,000 spring greens the other day because they were going to be ploughed back into the field. I couldn't have them because I didn't have anywhere to put them. I was offered ten tonnes of tomatoes from Kent because they were too big for Tesco."

The inquiry found that food banks worked well as a short-term "buffer zone" that helps people deal with temporary crises. But it says that most evidence submitted accepted that charity food aid alone was not a long-term solution, echoing this submission, by the Catholic Church:

"The aim should be to achieve food security for all in the UK. Household food security may be defined as households having adequate resources and access to be able to buy healthy, affordable food at all times."

Drawn from An Evidence Review for the All-Party Parliamentary Inquiry into Hunger in the United Kingdom, *by Andrew Forsey.*

8 December 2014

⇨ The above information is reprinted with kind permission from *The Guardian*. Please visit www.theguardian.com for further information.

11 facts about global poverty

1. Nearly half of the world's population – more than 3 billion people – live on less than $2.50 a day. More than 1.3 billion live in extreme poverty – less than $1.25 a day.

2. One billion children worldwide are living in poverty. According to UNICEF, 22,000 children die each day due to poverty.

3. 805 million people worldwide do not have enough food to eat. Food banks are especially important in providing food for people that can't afford it themselves. Run a food drive outside your local grocery store so people in your community have enough to eat. Sign up for Supermarket Stakeout.

4. More than 750 million people lack adequate access to clean drinking water. Diarrhoea caused by inadequate drinking water, sanitation and hand hygiene kills an estimated 842,000 people every year globally, or approximately 2,300 people per day.

5. In 2011, 165 million children under the age of five were stunted (reduced rate of growth and development) due to chronic malnutrition.

6. Preventable diseases like diarrhoea and pneumonia take the lives of two million children a year who are too poor to afford proper treatment.

7. As of 2013, 21.8 million children under one year of age worldwide had not received the three recommended doses of vaccine against diphtheria, tetanus and pertussis.

8. One quarter of all humans live without electricity – approximately 1.6 billion people.

9. 80% of the world population lives on less than $10 a day.

10. Oxfam estimates that it would take $60 billion annually to end extreme global poverty – that's less than one quarter the income of the top 100 richest billionaires.

11. The World Food Programme says, "The poor are hungry and their hunger traps them in poverty." Hunger is the number one cause of death in the world, killing more than HIV/AIDS, malaria and tuberculosis combined.

Sources

1 United Nations Development Programme. "Sustaining Human Progress: Reducing Vulnerabilities and Building Resilience." Human Development Report, 2014. Web Accessed February 25, 2015.

2 United Nations Inter-agency Group for Child Mortality Estimation (UN IGME). "UNICEF: Committing to Child Survival: A promise renewed." UNICEF, 2014. Web Accessed February 25, 2015.

3 FAO, IFAD and WFP. "The State of Food Insecurity in the World 2014. Strengthening the enabling environment for food security and nutrition." Food and Agriculture Organization of the UN, 2014. Web Accessed February 25, 2015.

4 World Health Organization and UNICEF Joint Monitoring Programme (JMP). "Progress on Drinking Water and Sanitation, 2014 Update." 2014. Web Accessed February 25, 2015.

5 United Nations Children's Fund (UNICEF). "IMPROVING CHILD NUTRITION: The achievable imperative for global progress." United Nations Children's Fund. 2013. Web Accessed February 25, 2015.

6 United Nations Children's Fund (UNICEF) . "Pneumonia and diarrhoea Tackling the deadliest diseases for the world's poorest children." Web accessed February 25, 2014,

7 UNICEF and WHO. "Immunization Summary: A statistical reference containing data through 2013." 10 November 2014. Web Accessed 25 February 2015.

8 United Nations. "The Millennium Development Goals Report 2007." United Nations, 2007. Web Accessed April 29, 2014.

9 Ravallion, Martin, Shaohua Chen, and Prem Sangraula. Dollar a Day Revisited. Working paper no. 4620. The World Bank, May 2008. Web Accessed February 25, 2014.

10 Oxfam. "The cost of inequality: how wealth and income extremes hurt us all." Oxfam, 2013. Web Accessed May 6, 2014.

11 World Food Programme. "What causes hunger?" Food Programme Fighting Hunger Worldwide, 2010. Web Accessed February 22, 2014.

⇨ The above information is reprinted with kind permission from Do Something. Please visit www.dosomething.org for further information.

Why the title of "developing country" no longer exists

By Matthew Lynn

They are exploited by ruthless multi-nationals. They are under the jackboot of champagne-swilling currency traders. They are in hock to the banks, crushed by unfair trade agreements, and their workers are virtual slaves, turning out clothes in sweatshops on starvation wages. To many people on the Left, vast parts of the world are impoverished by a greedy West, while the professional poverty industry insists that the world is becoming more and more unequal all the time.

But here is a strange thing. The World Bank has just decided to get rid of the term "developing countries". Why? Because these countries have become so successful, the World Bank has decided the term no longer has any real meaning. On the measures that actually count, such as infant mortality, life expectancy, educational standards or public health, there isn't much difference any more between the "developed" and "developing" world. Those differences that do remain are more likely to be within countries than between them.

The change has been achieved through free markets, competition and more open and more liberal trade. Capitalism has worked remarkably well for most of what used to be regarded as the third world. It is about time that the Left, and indeed a lot of mainstream liberal opinion, caught up to the way that the global economy has changed – instead of constantly ramping up the rhetoric about how evil the West is.

When you look at the actual numbers, many of the traditional divisions turn out to be way past their sell-by date. In its 2016 update of its Development Indices, the World Bank decided to get rid of the distinction between the "developing" world, defined as low and middle-income nations, and "developed" world, defined as high-income nations, across its whole range of statistics and programmes. The reason for that decision was fascinating. "There is no longer a distinction," it concluded.

On most crucial measures, that is certainly true. Take infant mortality and fertility rates, for example, which are often used as a proxy for the over-all wellbeing of a country. In 1960, there was a clear divide between a large group of counties where people had lots of babies, and a lot of them died, and a much smaller group where people had far fewer children, but almost all of them survived. Fast-forward to today, and pretty much every country has the same record.

Most countries in what had been classified as the developing world have made huge progress, and closed most of the gap. The World Bank cites the example of Mexico, which now has a gross national income (GNI) per capita of $9,860. It is ridiculous to bundle it in with a genuinely poor country such as Malawi, with a GNI of $250. Likewise, relatively few Mexicans are living in what the Bank regards as "absolute poverty" – less than 3% of that country's population are below that level.

Indeed, when you take the Bank's overall measures of absolute poverty, which include such factors as having enough to eat, clean water, basic sanitation, access to reasonable healthcare, education, affordable energy and so on, there was no longer a meaningful distinction to be made between the developed and the developing world. The real differences are now more likely to be within particular countries.

We can see that even in this country – Glasgow now has a significantly lower male life expectancy than Vietnam (71 years against 75, in case you were wondering), but it doesn't make much sense to re-classify Britain as a "developing" country just because some bits are very poor. There are similar pockets of deprivation within most advanced economies.

For all the talk of global poverty and inequality, the world has been making remarkable progress towards higher levels of prosperity. Take the World Bank's extreme poverty measure, which it defines as living on less than $1.90 a day. 30 years ago, that covered close on 40% of the world's

population. Now it is less than 10%. That is a dramatic shift in a relatively short period of time.

In the main, that has been driven by open markets, freer trade and more competition – in other words by liberal capitalism. The American think-tank the Cato Institute has a remarkable graph showing the decline of poverty on one axis and the rise of economic freedom – as measured by declining levels of state control, the ending of restrictions on trade and the enforcement of property rights – on the other. As economic freedom has risen, so poverty has declined, and that is true right across the world. From the collapse of communism in Russia and Eastern Europe, to the reforms in China, to the opening up of markets by successive trade agreements, to the free flow of people, goods and capital, and the globalisation of manufacturing, the entire world has made huge strides since the 1980s.

Many people in the poverty industry have tried to shift the goal posts by focusing on ownership of capital – always a lot less evenly distributed than income – or else by redefining poverty as "relative" rather than absolute, which means that just about all of us are always going to be poor compared to the people working at Goldman Sachs or Facebook. And yet those efforts are failing, and deservedly so.

The World Bank's decision is just the latest example of that. Semantics matter. The titles of developed and developing world reinforce the sense that the global economy is split between the haves and the have-nots. The reality is very different. As long as we keep liberalising markets, the gap will close even more – so much so that the very idea of a "developing" world can be consigned to the dustbin.

23 May 2016

⇨ The above information is reprinted with kind permission from *The Telegraph*. Please visit www.telegraph.co.uk for further information.

Hunger statistics

From the World Food Programme.

⇨ Some 795 million people in the world do not have enough food to lead a healthy active life. That's about one in nine people on Earth.(1)

⇨ The vast majority of the world's hungry people live in developing countries, where 12.9% of the population is undernourished.(2)

⇨ Asia is the continent with the most hungry people – two-thirds of the total. The percentage in southern Asia has fallen in recent years but in western Asia it has increased slightly.(3)

⇨ Sub-Saharan Africa is the region with the highest prevalence (percentage of population) of hunger. One person in four there is undernourished.(4)

⇨ Poor nutrition causes nearly half (45%) of deaths in children under five – 3.1 million children each year. (5)

⇨ One out of six children – roughly 100 million – in developing countries is underweight.(6)

⇨ One in four of the world's children are stunted. In developing countries the proportion can rise to one in three.(7)

⇨ If women farmers had the same access to resources as men, the number of hungry in the world could be reduced by up to 150 million.(8)

⇨ 66 million primary school-age children attend classes hungry across the developing world, with 23 million in Africa alone.(9)

⇨ WFP calculates that US$3.2 billion is needed per year to reach all 66 million hungry school-age children.(10)

Sources

1. *State of Food Insecurity in the World*, FAO, 2015

2. *State of Food Insecurity in the World*, FAO, 2015

3. *State of Food Insecurity in the World*, FAO, 2015

4. *State of Food Insecurity in the World*, FAO, 2015

5. *Series on Maternal and Child Nutrition*, The Lancet, 2013

6. *Global Health Observatory*, WHO, 2012

7. *Prevalence and Trends of Stunting among ... Children*, Public Health Nutrition, 2012

8. *Women in Agriculture: Closing the Gender Gap for Development*, FAO, 2011

9. *Two Minutes to Learn About School Meals*, WFP, 2012

10. *Two Minutes to Learn About School Meals*, WFP, 2012

⇨ The above information is reprinted with kind permission from the World Food Programme. Please visit www.wfp.org for further information.

Some 795 million people in the world do not have enough food to lead a healthy active life.

That's about one in nine people on Earth.

Source: State of Food Insecurity in the World, FAO, 2015.

We've reached the end of the Millennium Development Goals period – so, are children better off?

An article from The Conversation.

THE C🔿NVERSATION

By Jo Boyden, Professor of International Development and Director, Young Lives, University of Oxford

The 15-year period set out to achieve the UN's Millennium Development Goals (MDGs) has come to an end. Before we head straight into a new set of 17 targets – the Global Goals for 2030 – we still have to consider how well we met the old promises made back in 2000.

At the University of Oxford's Young Lives project we've been working on a report analysing the results of our ongoing study of 12,000 children born before and after the new millennium in four countries: Ethiopia, India, Peru and Vietnam. It's a 15-year study to overlap with the time-frame of the MDGs, providing evidence and policy advice on the most effective ways to tackle childhood poverty. So what did the MDGS do for our group of children?

Since 2000, the economic situation in all four of the countries has improved. According to the World Bank, between 1995 and 2010,

per capita Gross National Income (GNI) grew by 91% in Ethiopia, 122% in India, 61% in Peru and 145% in Vietnam. And, using the MDG definition of poverty as the percentage of the population living on less than a dollar a day, overall levels of poverty have fallen in all four countries.

What has economic growth brought?

Most of the families in the Young Lives study are poor, or relatively poor. On the whole, the economic growth means they have become less poor, despite the global financial crisis and a widespread rise in food prices. Over the past 15 years, there has been a pattern of generally rising living standards, with many of our families noticing improvements in their homes and communities. They now have greater access to consumer goods, and services such as electricity, safe water, sanitation and roads, though there have been smaller gains in housing quality. Overall levels of stunting – low height-for-age which is a sign of under-nutrition – have also fallen.

Louam, age nine, who lives in Ethiopia, feels her family's situation has certainly improved. Her village has a new road, a new bridge, a school, a health centre and a church – and some people now have mobile phones, though her family does not. "We have built a kitchen and a toilet, so we no longer have to go outside," Louam says. "We have tap water, but no power supply."

Yet as with the MDGs in general, progress for families involved in the Young Lives study has been uneven. Often, it is the children from better-off families who have experienced the greater gains. As a result, inequalities are more entrenched and disadvantages are increasingly concentrated among the most marginalised children.

The poorest families, who have benefited least from economic growth, face the greatest risks. These can be economic, such as rises in food prices that lead them to cut back on meals; environmental, such as droughts, that cause their harvests to fail; or health-related, such as repeated bouts of illness. And these are the families with the fewest resources to cope, throwing into sharp relief the need for social protection policies.

Hung is 17 and lives in rural Vietnam. A few years ago, his family lost its entire crop of oranges following a flood. Two years later, they lost their pigs to foot-and-mouth disease. "We had 45 pigs. They were very big and as long as a shoulder pole (yoke)," says Hung's mother, who comes from a poor family of eight children. "I burst into tears when counting how little money we earned that year."

Then, Hung's brother, who has never been healthy, fell ill and needed surgery, which was both worrying and costly. Hung dropped out of school and started looking for a job, finally finding work with a construction company. He still has hopes for the future, but is reluctant to talk about them. "I'm afraid that if I talk about my dream, it would never come true," he says. An employment guarantee scheme or health insurance might have prevented Hung from leaving school and supported him to achieve his aspirations.

The gaps are growing wider

The gap between rich and poor is growing, but so too are the gaps between rural and urban areas, ethnic majority and ethnic minority children and in India, between different caste groups. Disparities between boys and girls remain. These different forms of inequality interact and intersect, meaning the same children often face multiple disadvantages: on the basis of where they live, what ethnic group they come from, and whether they are girls or boys.

So we find that the poorest children in all four countries are as likely as ever to be stunted, and that the poorest children and those in rural areas are still the least likely to have access to safe water and sanitation. The gaps began to emerge earlier than we had first imagined – children are falling behind before they have even started school, and the new phenomenon of low-fee private education is serving to widen the gulf, as well as exacerbating gender-based inequalities. The poorest children are the most likely to drop out of school after the age of 15, and girls from poor and rural families are the most likely to marry and have their first child while still in their teens.

The MDGs have been an important catalyst for change, prompting the introduction of many valuable pro-poor social interventions and policies, which have seen widespread gains in terms of nutrition, health and education. One such example is India's midday schools meal scheme which has been remarkably successful, not only in improving primary school children's nutrition but also increasing educational enrolment, retention and attendance.

But there is clearly still a long way to go to tackle the root causes of poverty and inequality and above all, for children, on whom future development and economic growth depend.

The next 15 years

Now the MDGs have been put to bed, the Global Goals for 2030, focus on poverty and inequality as a problem that needs tackling at global as well as regional, national and sub-national levels. But there are some key challenges that remain unsolved.

These include making sure we plan for human development and wellbeing across the course of people's lives. In particular, we need to develop better policies to support the critical first 1,000 days of life. School enrolment also needs to be converted into learning success, so that the poorest children are prevented from being behind even before they start in the classroom.

The structural sources of disadvantage for women, such as their limited options in the labour market, still too easily shape their decision making. In the future, governments need to provide the skills, as well as the jobs, to capitalise on the demographic dividend of a rising youth population. Citizens must rally round to stoke the political will necessary to increase social protection measures that effectively make a difference to children's outcomes.

The emphasis on environmental sustainability, which matters a lot for the children in our sample, with Ethiopia and Peru among the countries most affected globally by climate change, is critical. It is probably the single greatest challenge to current and future generations of children.

By the time these new Global Goals are deemed a success or failure, the cohorts in our study will be describing their millennium childhoods to their own adolescent children. Let's hope that the changes we anticipate are so great, their children will find these stories incredulous.

31 December 2015

⇨ The above information is reprinted with kind permission from *The Conversation*. Please visit www.theconversation.com for further information.

The poor and hungry should not be punished for stealing food, Italian court rules

By Sara C Nelson

Italy's top criminal court has ruled that a hungry homeless man who took a package of hot dogs from a supermarket committed no crime.

Roman Ostriakov had been about to leave the store after paying for breadsticks but not for the hot dogs and some cheese worth €4.07 he had in his pocket.

He was convicted of theft, and sentenced by a lower court in Genoa to six months in prison and a €100 fine, the Associated Press reports.

The Rome-based Cassation Court on Monday ruled that Ostriakov had taken the food "in the face of the immediate and essential need for nourishment" and that it was therefore not a crime.

A columnist in Turin newspaper *La Stampa* wrote Tuesday the high court's ruling "reminds everyone that in a civilized country not even the worst of men can die of hunger".

Citing the ruling, Italiaglobale.it declared it "right" and "pertinent", continuing that it derives from a concept that "informed the Western world for centuries, it is called humanity".

4 May 2016

⇨ The above information is reprinted with kind permission from *The Huffington Post UK*. Please visit www.huffingtonpost.co.uk for further information.

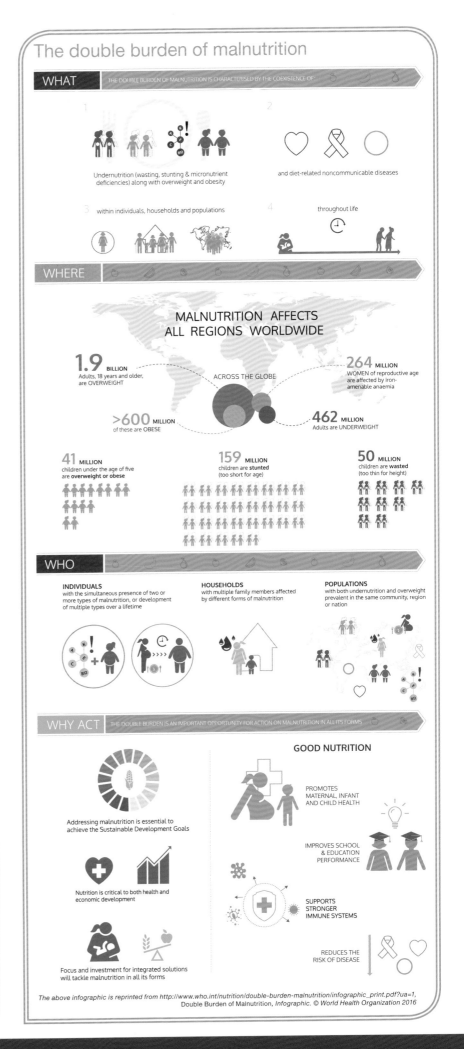

The double burden of malnutrition

WHAT — THE DOUBLE BURDEN OF MALNUTRITION IS CHARACTERISED BY THE COEXISTENCE OF:

1 Undernutrition (wasting, stunting & micronutrient deficiencies) along with overweight and obesity

2 and diet-related noncommunicable diseases

3 within individuals, households and populations

4 throughout life

WHERE

MALNUTRITION AFFECTS ALL REGIONS WORLDWIDE

1.9 BILLION Adults, 18 years and older, are OVERWEIGHT

ACROSS THE GLOBE

264 MILLION WOMEN of reproductive age are affected by iron-amenable anaemia

>600 MILLION of these are OBESE

462 MILLION Adults are UNDERWEIGHT

41 MILLION children under the age of five are overweight or obese

159 MILLION children are stunted (too short for age)

50 MILLION children are wasted (too thin for height)

WHO

INDIVIDUALS with the simultaneous presence of two or more types of malnutrition, or development of multiple types over a lifetime

HOUSEHOLDS with multiple family members affected by different forms of malnutrition

POPULATIONS with both undernutrition and overweight prevalent in the same community, region or nation

WHY ACT — THE DOUBLE BURDEN IS AN IMPORTANT OPPORTUNITY FOR ACTION ON MALNUTRITION IN ALL ITS FORMS

Addressing malnutrition is essential to achieve the Sustainable Development Goals

Nutrition is critical to both health and economic development

Focus and investment for integrated solutions will tackle malnutrition in all its forms

GOOD NUTRITION

PROMOTES MATERNAL, INFANT AND CHILD HEALTH

IMPROVES SCHOOL & EDUCATION PERFORMANCE

SUPPORTS STRONGER IMMUNE SYSTEMS

REDUCES THE RISK OF DISEASE

The above infographic is reprinted from http://www.who.int/nutrition/double-burden-malnutrition/infographic_print.pdf?ua=1, Double Burden of Malnutrition, Infographic. © World Health Organization 2016

Meet the kids scavenging on rubbish dumps to survive

Shockingly, 15 million people in the developing world today survive by salvaging waste. Many of them are children. We lift the lid on the worldwide scandal of young kids forced to scavenge on rubbish dumps to survive.

By Renata Watson

Meet Margaret, from Kenya. Margaret lives with her family on the Mwakirunge dumpsite just outside Mombasa. Every day she wades through rubbish, broken glass and toxic waste, collecting scrap metal and plastic to sell to earn a living. She is ten years old.

Margaret told us: "It is very dirty and there is a bad smell. I know there are very bad diseases that I can catch here. I am afraid of being cut by broken bottles, nails or syringes. There are some men who go round beating people with bottles when they are drunk."

Margaret is just one of the hundreds of girls who are forced to work here every day. Children are missing out on school so they can contribute to the family's income.

But they don't earn much. Middlemen buy recyclables recovered by the waste pickers, and sort, clean and process them before selling to scrap dealers who sell it on. It's these middlemen and scrap dealers who often earn large profits.

In Sierra Leone, a country recovering from decades of civil war – and more recently in the epicentre of the worst ever Ebola outbreak in history – the capital, Freetown has a massive rubbish dump right in the middle of the city. When British TV actress Sarah Alexander visited it she told us: "It's hell on Earth."

During the rainy season, the residents, who live on the edge of the dump, try to earn a living from scouring through rotting rubbish, plastic bags and raw sewage for discarded things they can sell.

As well as the daily grind for survival, people living on dumps often face discrimination. When you live and work on a rubbish dump everything about you is permeated by the overpowering smell. It identifies you before you even open your mouth as someone who lives outside of 'normal' society.

Dumpsite life also means women and girls are vulnerable to violence and sexual abuse, even rape – but because people are so poor and on the fringes of society there is nowhere for them to go for healthcare or support.

Children belong in school, not on rubbish dumps

This isn't "just" happening in Sierra Leone and Kenya. All over the world – China, Brazil, India – you'll find people picking rubbish, in horrible conditions.

ActionAid is helping girls and women waste pickers to stand up to sexual exploitation and discrimination. And we're working with children like Margaret to get them off the dump and into school.

It takes time and money. And that's where child sponsorship comes in. We know it's one of the best ways to help children escape poverty, give them the chance of an education, and to give their whole community hope for the future.

30 January 2015

⇨ The above information is reprinted with kind permission from ActionAid. Please visit www.actionaid.org.uk for further information.

Was there ever a time when so few people controlled so much wealth?

An article from **The Conversation.**

THE CONVERSATION

By Eoin Flaherty, Lecturer in Sociology, Queen's University Belfast

Oxfam's latest report claims that income inequality has reached a new global extreme, exceeding even its predictions from the previous year. The figures behind this claim are striking – just 62 individuals now hold the same wealth as the bottom half of humanity, compared to 80 in 2014 and 388 in 2010. It appears not only has the financial crisis been weathered by the global elite, but that their fortunes have collectively improved.

Our objections to inequality, the report notes, are not driven simply by a desire to improve our own material standard of living. Rising inequality is one of the surest signs of the failure of economic growth to make things better for us all. The accompanying decline in the income shares of the bottom 50% since 2010 suggests that although governments across the world have been quick to tout their role in bringing about a global 'recovery', its rewards have been very selectively spread.

It would be foolish to pretend that wealth inequality is a product of the liberal capitalism of the past couple of hundred years. Peppered throughout recorded history are examples of exceptional wealth deriving from the spoils of empire and warfare – the Roman emperor Caesar Augustus is thought to have controlled the equivalent of $4.6 trillion – one fifth of the total wealth of the empire. The richest man in history, according to *Time* magazine was Mansa Musa, the king of Timbuktu – who ruled from 1280 to 1337 when his kingdom was the biggest producer of gold in the world. His wealth, says *Time*, is beyond calculation: "richer than anyone could describe".

Historical figures show how important military and legal force was for wealth accumulation, from the lands of Genghis Khan in the 13th century (once the largest empire in history), to Chinese emperor Shenzong, who possessed up to 30% of global GDP at the height of his power in the 11th century.

Wealth accumulation in non-capitalistic societies was often predicated on forced seizure – a process known as 'primitive accumulation'. The most famous instance was the English enclosure movement of the 18th and 19th centuries, which paved the way for the expansion of many great landed estates.

Learning greed

But is inequality inevitable in human society? In the late 19th century, evolutionary anthropologists such as Henry Maine and Lewis Morgan suggested that the human societies of their time may have evolved from less complex forms of clan-based societies, into more complex class-based societies. And in 2009, Elinor Ostrom was awarded the Nobel Prize for her work on 'common-pool' systems – societies in which resources were pooled for the good of the community, often at odds with our modern conception of private property.

Ostrom's work demonstrated that, where conditions were favourable, these systems, such as fisheries, irrigation systems, common grazing and forests, thrived – perhaps better than similar systems maintained through top-down organisation. Discussion continues today as to whether these forms of social organisation were widespread throughout much of human history and whether our more 'unequal' forms of modern society may have evolved from this egalitarian base.

The jury is also very much out on the question of whether human societies have always been capitalist. While many argue that certain features of capitalist societies were present throughout all of human history (Adam Smith's famous statement on the human propensity to "truck, barter, and trade") the institutions which together make up modern capitalism were not.

In feudal societies of the Middle Ages for example, the ability of any individual to accumulate material wealth was largely constrained by the amount of 'things' they could reasonably possess. While there were forms of credit and developed money systems, there

were nonetheless some 'absolute' limits on what one could physically amass (usually depending on direct coercion).

Paper money

Today, the accumulation of wealth does not depend solely on material goods, or claims on real assets such as property, means of production such as industrial plant and infrastructure – or indeed people (in the US during slave-owning days the possession of slaves constituted a sizeable portion of one's capital).

Economist Thomas Piketty points out that much wealth in classical literature seems to derive from rent-generating property in the hands of a limited number of people. But today, our fractional reserve banking systems mean that much of our money supply does not exist in physical form. Paper money is just a small portion of a bank's balance sheet, with liabilities in the form of debt constituting much of the remainder.

One of the chief innovations of the last century, and indeed one of the key culprits involved in rising inequality identified by Oxfam, is the growth of an industry of tradable intangible assets in the

form of financial instruments. Indeed, deregulation of the financial industry has been one of the most significant processes feeding into rising inequality in recent years.

The years after the great depression of the 1930s were also ones of regulatory reform. The US Glass-Steagall Act of 1933 kept commercial and investment banking largely separate, while tight controls were maintained on foreign transactions in many European countries.

But much of this was swept away during the late 20th century. Before the financial crisis, the repackaging of high-risk mortgages and their subsequent trading on financial markets, offered an ideal opportunity for capital-endowed investors to make sizeable profits while ultimately hedging the immediate risk onto homeowners. Little is today beyond the reach of investment markets, from mortgages to carbon emissions, to speculation on the future performances of companies. Whether or not the world has ever been as unequal before, we can at least say that the opportunities for wealth accumulation today are radically different from those of the past.

Time to take back control?

Part of the problem in establishing precisely whether the world has ever been as unequal is that we simply lack the data. The best estimates derive from the World Top Incomes study, the earliest of which for the UK dates to 1918. On this basis at least – where data can be compared between countries and where methods of calculation are standardised – we can say that things have scarcely been this unequal since before World War II.

But we should not compare on the basis of value alone. After all, we can scarcely argue that life under the direct coercion of feudalism, or wealth generated through the exploitation of natural resources by colonising empires was much preferable. But a backward glance through human history does confront some common myths about the society we inhabit today. Ours is not the only historical form of social organisation, nor is the current economic order beyond our control.

If we can clearly identify how decisions taken by governments around taxation or financial regulation, for example, have facilitated rising wealth inequality, then we can be ever more certain that society has the potential to change this. Knowing the factors that continue to drive inequality today – and the myths which claim the world must inevitably be this way – means we can also challenge it.

27 January 2016

⇨ The above information is reprinted with kind permission from *The Conversation*. Please visit www.theconversation.com for further information.

The global wealth pyramid

Wealth range	Number of adults (percent of world population)	Total wealth (percent of world)
> USD 1 million	34 m (0.7%)	USD 112.9 trn (45.2%)
USD 100,000 to 1 million	349 m (7.4%)	USD 98.5 trn (39.4%)
USD 10,000 to 100,000	1,003 m (21.0%)	USD 131.3 trn (12.5%)
< USD 10,000	3,386 m (71.0%)	USD 7.4 trn (3.0%)

Source: James Davies, Rodrigo Lluberas and Anthony Sharrocks, Credit Suisse Global Wealth Databook 2015

Chapter 3

Eradicating poverty

Poverty eradication

Eradicating poverty in all its forms and dimensions, including extreme poverty, is the greatest global challenge and an indispensable requirement for sustainable development.

The 2030 Agenda for Sustainable Development resolves to free the human race from the tyranny of poverty and to heal and secure our planet.

The first Sustainable Development Goal aims to "End poverty in all its forms everywhere". Its seven associated targets aims, among others, to eradicate extreme poverty for all people everywhere, reduce at least by half the proportion of men, women and children of all ages living in poverty, and implement nationally appropriate social protection systems and measures for all, including floors, and by 2030 achieve substantial coverage of the poor and the vulnerable.

As recalled by the foreword of the 2015 *Millennium Development Goals Report*, at the Millennium Summit in September 2000, 189 countries unanimously adopted the Millennium Declaration, pledging to "spare no effort to free our fellow men, women and children from the abject and dehumanizing conditions of extreme poverty". This commitment was translated into an inspiring framework of eight goals and, then, into wide-ranging practical steps that have enabled people across the world to improve their lives and their future prospects. The MDGs helped to lift more than one billion people out of extreme poverty, to make inroads against hunger, to enable more girls to attend school than ever before and to protect our planet.

Nevertheless, in spite of all the remarkable gains, inequalities have persisted and progress has been uneven. Therefore, the 2030 Agenda for Sustainable Development and its set of Sustainable Development Goals have been committed, as stated in the Declaration of the Agenda, "to build upon the achievements of the Millennium Development Goals and seek to address their unfinished business".

From Agenda 21 to Future We Want

In 'The Future We Want', the outcome document of Rio+20, Member States emphasised the need to accord the highest priority to poverty eradication within the United Nations development agenda, addressing the root causes and challenges of poverty through integrated, coordinated and coherent strategies at all levels.

In the context of the multi-year programme of work adopted by the Commission on Sustainable Development (CSD) after the 2002 World Summit on Sustainable Development (WSSD), poverty eradication appears as an "overriding issue" on the agenda of the CSD each year.

Poverty eradication is addressed in Chapter II of the *Johannesburg Plan of Implementation* (2002), which stressed that eradicating poverty is the greatest global challenge facing the world today and an indispensable requirement for sustainable development, particularly for developing countries.

Priority actions on poverty eradication include:

⇨ improving access to sustainable livelihoods, entrepreneurial opportunities and productive resources;

⇨ providing universal access to basic social services;

⇨ progressively developing social protection systems to support those who cannot support themselves;

- ⇨ empowering people living in poverty and their organisations;
- ⇨ addressing the disproportionate impact of poverty on women;
- ⇨ working with interested donors and recipients to allocate increased shares of ODA to poverty eradication; and
- ⇨ intensifying international cooperation for poverty eradication.

The General Assembly, in its 1997 Programme for the Further Implementation of Agenda 21 (paragraph 27) decided that poverty eradication should be an overriding theme of sustainable development for the coming years. It is one of the fundamental goals of the international community and of the entire United Nations system.

'Combating poverty' is the topic of Chapter 3 of Agenda 21. It is also in commitment 2 of the Copenhagen Declaration on Social Development.

Agenda 21 emphasised that poverty is a complex multidimensional problem with origins in both the national and international domains. No uniform solution can be found for global application. Rather, country-specific programmes to tackle poverty and international efforts supporting national efforts, as well as the parallel process of creating a supportive international environment, are crucial for a solution to this problem.

The years following the 1992 Rio Conference have witnessed an increase in the number of people living in absolute poverty, particularly in developing countries. The enormity and complexity of the poverty issue could endanger the social fabric, undermine economic development and the environment, and threaten political stability in many countries.

- ⇨ The above information is from the Sustainable Development Knowledge Platform. © 2016 United Nations. Reprinted with permission of the United Nations. Visit sustainabledevelopment. un.org for further information.

Give children free meals during school holidays to stop them starving, teachers urge

Some pupils have to go without food on a "daily basis", according to one teacher.

Children should be given free meals during the summer holidays to avoid them starving during the seven-week break from school, teachers have declared.

Delegates at the Association of Teachers and Lecturers' conference in Liverpool warned poorer pupils could suffer a drop-off in learning as a result of not eating properly during the summer break.

A poll of more than 400 teachers revealed four out of ten believed they had pupils in their school who relied on food banks to feed them. Almost half (49 per cent) felt a lack of food during the long summer break adversely affected pupils' mental health.

The poll revealed that 15 per cent of teaching staff brought in their own food to feed pupils whose families were just above the poverty line and therefore not entitled to free school meals during term time. A further 15 per cent regularly offered to buy food for the pupils.

Niamh Sweeney, from Cambridgeshire, told the conference: "The levels of poverty and hunger I see today reflect those from the early 20th century."

She said that some people had to go without food "on an almost daily basis", adding: "it is an utter horror that something needs to be done at all".

John Puckrin, from inner London, said figures showed a 21 per cent increase in demand for food banks during the summer holidays.

"For many the school holidays provide a chance to relax and enjoy new experiences, meeting new people, going to places perhaps different cultures and languages – the chance to grow their cultural capital or improve their sporting skills," he added. "But for the poorest it is often a closed isolating experience and a lack of any positive stimulation."

Dr Mary Bousted, general secretary of ATL, added: "The effect of hunger on pupils' learning is evident and it is shocking that in the 21st century so many pupils still come to school hungry with no means to buy lunch.

"With many families having to rely on charities such as food bank hand-outs, we risk returning to a Victorian era rife with inequality."

She said it was "encouraging" that the Government had earmarked £10 million to help schools establish breakfast clubs for pupils from September but added: "This is just a drop in the ocean for the thousands of pupils who miss out on breakfast and aren't entitled to free school meals because they are from a low-income working family."

5 April 2016

- ⇨ The above information is reprinted with kind permission from *The Independent*. Please visit www.independent.co.uk for further information.

© independent.co.uk 2016

Fee-free bank accounts launched

New Year boost for millions as fee-free bank accounts become available for first time.

Millions of bank customers across Britain stand to benefit by hundreds of pounds as nine major banks launch fee-free basic bank accounts from 1 January.

The accounts will be available to anyone who doesn't already have a bank account, is ineligible for a standard current account or who can't use their existing account due to financial difficulty.

For the first time they will be truly fee-free, helping people to manage their money without fear of running up an overdraft.

Today's (27 December 2015) announcement follows last Christmas' landmark agreement between the Government and the banking industry to establish new basic bank accounts that will end bank charges if a direct debit or standing order fails.

In some cases, charges had been as high as £35 per failed item, and uncapped, meaning charges could accumulate to hundreds of pounds over time and drive people into serious debt.

The changes will remove the risk that basic bank account customers will be forced into overdraft because of these fees and charges.

Basic bank account customers will now also be offered services on the same terms as other personal current accounts that the banks provides, including access to all the standard over-the-counter services at bank branches and at the Post Office, and access to the entire ATM network.

Existing basic bank account customers should ask their bank whether they could still be charged if a direct debit or standing order fails, and whether they are eligible for a new basic bank account.

There are an estimated nine million basic bank accounts in the UK.

Economic Secretary Harriett Baldwin said:

"Making sure that everyone in Britain has access to basic banking and financial services is at the heart of our long-term plan.

"That's why I'm delighted that for the first time, truly fee-free basic bank accounts will be available to anyone who doesn't already have an account, or isn't able to use their existing account due to financial difficulty.

"This is a key step forward in ensuring that our banking industry works for everyone."

Sian Williams, Head of the Financial Health Exchange at Toynbee Hall, said:

"We know from our work with the financially excluded that a transactional bank account is essential for getting and sustaining a job and a home, as well as for accessing opportunities to study and take part in wider society. We therefore fully support the new Basic Bank Account initiative to ensure everyone has access to a bank account.

"We particularly welcome the commitment that the poorest and most vulnerable customers will be protected from the account fees and charges which can unintentionally lead to self-exclusion or unmanageable debt.

"We are confident that these new accounts will play a significant role in reducing the number of unbanked and underbanked individuals even further, and we look forward to working with the banking sector and HM Treasury to monitor the implementation of the new account standards and to seeing the difference they will make for some of the most vulnerable in our society."

The banks and building societies that have signed up to offer a basic bank account from 1 January 2016 and their corresponding bank account product are:

⇨ Barclays – Barclays Basic Current Account

⇨ Santander – Basic Current Account

⇨ NatWest – Foundation Account

⇨ Ulster Bank (Northern Ireland) – Foundation Account

⇨ The Royal Bank of Scotland (Scotland) – Foundation Account

⇨ RBS England and Wales – Basic Account

⇨ HSBC – Basic Bank Account

⇨ Nationwide – FlexBasic

⇨ Co-operative Bank – Cashminder

⇨ Lloyds Banking Group (including Halifax and Bank of Scotland brands) – Basic Account

⇨ TSB – Cash Account

⇨ National Australia Bank Group (including Yorkshire Bank and Clydesdale brands) – Readycash Account.

27 December 2015

⇨ The above information is reprinted with kind permission from GOV.UK.

Is this the generation that eradicates extreme poverty?

The year 2015 was a once in a generation event for the world's citizens and for the planet. In one year, a new blueprint was created to tackle the world's thorniest issues. Issues that affect all of us, like climate change, sustainable development and natural disasters.

By Helen Clark

From the Sendai Framework for Disaster Risk Reduction to the Addis Ababa Action Agenda on Financing for Development, from the Sustainable Development Summit in New York to the climate conference in Paris, it was a year in which the United Nations, in the words of Secretary-General Ban Ki-moon, proved it is able "to deliver hope and healing to the world".

Do global agreements, like those mentioned above, matter?

Yes, they do.

In September, world leaders came together to unanimously agree to a new set of goals that would guide sustainable development for the next 15 years. The Sustainable Development Goals (SDGs) replace the previous goals, the Millennium Development Goals (MDGs).

The MDGs were created to tackle some of the most challenging issues then faced in development; eradicating poverty; enrolling children in school; ending hunger; turning the tide on HIV/AIDS, malaria and TB; and reducing infant, child and maternal deaths.

There has been significant progress in the areas targeted by the MDGs – progress which would have been unlikely without the focus, funding and action around these goals.

Yet there is also much unfinished business, and the new global development agenda must overcome some major challenges:

⇨ While the target of halving the proportion of people living in extreme poverty by 2015 was met, it is not much fun being in the other half – the so-called "bottom billion", for

many of whom life has scarcely changed.

⇨ Child poverty is rising in 18 out of 28 EU countries, and has been linked by the International Labour Organization to falling levels of maternal and child benefits. The era of austerity has not been kind to social protection systems in many countries.

⇨ Gender inequality remains pervasive – despite the fact that societies are the poorer if they fail to tap the full potential of half their population. Where women are 'out of sight, out of mind', disempowered and under-represented in decision-making circles, meeting their needs often isn't a priority.

⇨ The rapid pace of environmental degradation is damaging the ecosystems on which human survival and wellbeing depend. Species loss undermines livelihoods, health, and food and water security. While

the damage done to natural ecosystems affects us all, it does affect the poorest and most vulnerable the most.

⇨ There cannot be sustainable development without peace and stability – alas, right now the world suffers a big deficit in that respect.

Catastrophic emergencies created by war and conflict are overwhelming the international community's capacity to respond. Humanitarian relief spending has trebled in the last decade. On current trends there will never be enough money to meet the demand for relief.

It is critical that we work to reduce the demand for humanitarian support by investing in building more inclusive and peaceful societies and in disaster risk reduction. The new global agenda calls for access to justice for all, for accountable, inclusive and effective institutions at all levels, and for serious action to tackle inequalities.

The Sustainable Development Goals are universal goals, applying to countries at all stages of development. This highlights the fact that sustainable development in the 21st century isn't something that happens to somebody else, somewhere else. We all have a stake in it – and every country has work to do to progress towards it.

But the best agendas are mere words on paper unless they can be implemented.

The good news is that our world has more wealth, more knowledge and more technologies at its disposal than ever before. The challenges we face are mostly human induced. We can tackle them, but not if we keep doing business as usual and expecting different results.

Radical adjustments are needed in the way we live, work, produce, consume, generate our energy, transport ourselves and design our cities. There is capacity to be built. Governance to improve. Sweeping policy, legislative and regulatory changes are needed. A commitment to building lasting peace and stability based on peaceful and inclusive societies is essential.

Strong leadership at all levels is needed to realise the better world envisaged in the Sustainable Development Goals. First, leadership is needed on finding the funding required. Money isn't everything, but it certainly helps, including through Official Development Assistance.

Second, broad coalitions of leaders are needed. Clearly governments acting alone can't achieve the goals envisaged by the new global agenda. Their leadership is vital, but insufficient – broader leadership is also required. That includes leadership from civil society – from our NGOs, scientists, researchers and academia; and from local government and the private sector too.

Third, leadership is needed more than ever from the multilateral system – including from the United Nations Development Programme. Our job is to support countries to eradicate poverty, and to do that in a way that simultaneously reduces inequality and exclusion, and avoids wrecking the ecosystems on which life depends.

The new Sustainable Development Goals will guide development for the next 15 years, offering a chance to meet the global citizenry's aspirations for a more peaceful, prosperous and sustainable future.

Yet we will be striving to achieve the Global Goals at a time when volatility is the new normal. The realities of the world we live in must be acknowledged, and more pre-emptive investment must be made in risk-informed development:

⇨ The growing inequalities and unchecked discrimination which undermine social cohesion need to be tackled head on.

⇨ Environmental degradation must be arrested.

⇨ The downward spiral into conflict, instability, and crisis must be halted, and effective strategies based on building resilience must be adopted as ways of coping with protracted crises.

Ours is the last generation that can head off the worst effects of climate change. Postponed action will be too late. Ours is also the first generation that can eradicate extreme poverty and secure a more hopeful future for all. For this fearless leadership from us all is required.

Author: Helen Clark is the Administrator of the United Nations Development Programme and the former Prime Minister of New Zealand. She is participating in the World Economic Forum's Annual Meeting in Davos.

23 January 2016

⇨ The above information is reprinted with kind permission from the World Economic Forum and the UN. Please visit www.weforum.org for further information.

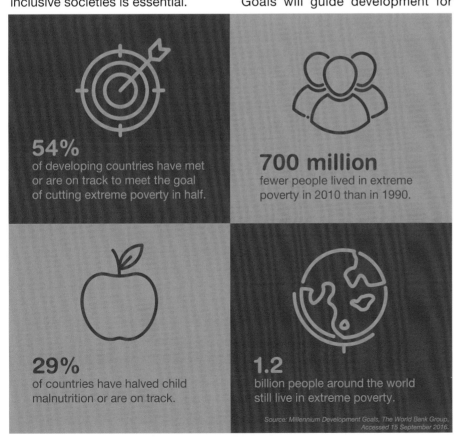

54%
of developing countries have met or are on track to meet the goal of cutting extreme poverty in half.

700 million
fewer people lived in extreme poverty in 2010 than in 1990.

29%
of countries have halved child malnutrition or are on track.

1.2
billion people around the world still live in extreme poverty.

Source: Millennium Development Goals, The World Bank Group, Accessed 15 September 2016.

Key facts

⇨ In 2007 UNICEF issued a report card on child wellbeing in rich countries, which brought together information on material conditions with other indicators such as health, education, peer and family relationships, behaviours and risks, and young people's own subjective sense of wellbeing. (page 1)

⇨ The UK has a very high level of income inequality compared to other developed countries. (page 2)

⇨ In the UK, households in the bottom 10% of the population have on average a net income of £9,277. The top 10% have net incomes over nine times that (£83,897). (page 2)

⇨ Wealth in Great Britain is even more unequally divided than income. The richest 10% of households hold 45% of all wealth. The poorest 50%, by contrast, own just 8.7%. (page 3)

⇨ Ten of the top 12 most declining UK cities are in the north of England. (page 6)

⇨ 27% of Londoners live in poverty after housing costs are taken into account, compared with 20% in the rest of England. The cost of housing is an important factor in London's higher poverty rate. (page 7)

⇨ The Debt Advisory Centre found that 4.7 million people across the UK are frequently cut off from their electricity supply, because they cannot afford to top-up pre-paid electricity meters. (page 8)

⇨ A household is in poverty if its income after tax and housing costs is less than 60% of the typical (median) household income. It therefore identifies poverty as those with an income considerably below what is typical in society. A single adult with a disposable income of less than £130 per week in 2012/13 would be in poverty. (page 10)

⇨ Of the 9.0 million young people aged 14–24 living in the UK, approximately 2.7 million, or 30%, are living in poverty. (page 10)

⇨ Six out of ten (59 per cent) vulnerable young people will not go into a bank for financial information or advice, saying they find them intimidating and unhelpful, according to a report published today by Action for Children. (page 12)

⇨ Many families living on a low income have only about £13 per day per person. (page 13)

⇨ There are currently 3.7 million children living in poverty in the UK. That's over a quarter of all children. 1.7 million of these children are living in severe poverty. In the UK 63% of children living in poverty are in a family where someone works. (page 13)

⇨ Analysis by the Health and Social Care Information Centre has found that one in six 15-year-olds in the UK who come from deprived areas reported having low life satisfaction, compared with around one in ten of those living in the least deprived areas. (page 15)

⇨ A study revealed 71% of parents found it harder to make ends meet during the summer holidays compared with term-time, while 63% of parents find themselves without enough money for food during the summer. A staggering 93% of low-income parents skip at least one meal a day to make sure their children are fed. (page 17)

⇨ According to the study by property experts Homewise, one in three over-60s said that cutbacks have lead to them borrowing money from friends and family and resorting to selling possessions because they do not have enough cash to live off. And one in ten have turned down the heating to save money and even started eating less in a bid to stave off poverty. (page 18)

⇨ 913,138 people received three days' emergency food from Trussell Trust food banks in 2013–14 compared to 346,992 in 2012–13. (page 20)

⇨ Nearly half of the world's population – more than 3 billion people – live on less than $2.50 a day. More than 1.3 billion live in extreme poverty – less than $1.25 a day. (page 26)

⇨ More than 750 million people lack adequate access to clean drinking water. Diarrhoea caused by inadequate drinking water, sanitation and hand hygiene kills an estimated 842,000 people every year globally, or approximately 2,300 people per day. (page 26)

⇨ Oxfam estimates that it would take $60 billion annually to end extreme global poverty – that's less than one quarter the income of the top 100 richest billionaires. (page 26)

⇨ Some 795 million people in the world do not have enough food to lead a healthy active life. That's about one in nine people on Earth. (page 28)

⇨ Shockingly, 15 million people in the developing world today survive by salvaging waste. (page 32)

⇨ Oxfam's latest report claims that income inequality has reached a new global extreme, exceeding even its predictions from the previous year. The figures behind this claim are striking – just 62 individuals now hold the same wealth as the bottom half of humanity, compared to 80 in 2014 and 388 in 2010. (page 33)

⇨ The 2030 Agenda for Sustainable Development resolves to free the human race from the tyranny of poverty and to heal and secure our planet. (page 35)

⇨ Millions of bank customers across Britain stand to benefit by hundreds of pounds as nine major banks launch fee-free basic bank accounts from 1 January. (page 37)

Absolute poverty

Inability to meet even the most basic survival needs. This includes life necessities such as food, water, shelter, clothing and health care.

Affluence

Wealth; abundance of money or valuable resources.

Benefits

We use the term 'state benefits' to describe any money that is given to us by the government. Benefits are paid to any member of the public, who may need extra money to help them meet the costs of everyday living.

Child poverty

In order to live above the poverty line, a family with two adults and two children in the UK needs £349 each week to cover food, transport, shoes, clothes, activities, electricity, gas, water, telephone bills, etc.

Developed country

Also known as a more developed country (MDC), a developed country has an advanced economy relative to other countries. In contrast with a developing country, MDCs tend to have higher rates of literacy, life expectancy and gross domestic product. Countries such as Germany and the United States are considered developed countries.

Developing country

Also known as a less-developed county (LDC), a developing country is a nation with a low quality of life and poor standard of living. The UN has come up with the Human Development Index which measures the development of a country by looking at rates of literacy, life expectancy, gross domestic product, etc. In LDCs these all tend to be lower in comparison to other countries. Countries such as Ethiopia and Afghanistan are considered developing countries.

Fuel poverty

A household is said to be in fuel poverty if they spend more than 10% of their income on heating their home.

Millennium Development Goals (MDG)

Agreed upon by 193 United Nations member states, the Millennium Development Goals are the world's targets for addressing poverty, education, disease, equality and environmental sustainability (made up of eight goals). For example, one goal is to eradicate extreme poverty and hunger. The aim was to achieve these goals by the year 2015. The MDGs are now replaced by the Sustainable Development Goals (SDGs).

Non-Governmental Organisation (NGO)

This abbreviation stands for non-governmental organisation. This refers to an organisation that operates independently and are not part of any government. They usually serve a wider social aim, that may have political aspects, and are primarily concerned with promoting a cause or helping with development projects. Oxfam and Red Cross are examples of NGOs.

Poverty

Peter Townsend offers this definition of poverty: 'Individuals, families and groups in the population can be said to be in poverty when they lack the resources to obtain the types of diet, participate in the activities, and have the living conditions and amenities which are customary, or are at least widely encouraged and approved, in the societies in which they belong.'

Poverty line

The poverty line is the income level below which an individual can be said to be living in poverty. In the UK, the poverty line is define as 60 per cent of median household income, adjusted for household composition. Globally speaking, people defined as living in absolute poverty if they have less than $1 (USD) a day to live on.

Recession

A period during which economic activity has slowed, causing a reduction in Gross Domestic Product (GDP), employment, household incomes and business profits. If GDP shows a reduction over at least six months, a country is then said to be in recession. Recessions are caused by people spending less, businesses making less and banks being more reluctant to give people loans.

Relative poverty

A measure of income inequality: dependent on social context, the standard of resources which is seen as socially acceptable in comparison with others in society. This differs between countries and over time. An income-related example would be living on less than X% of the average UK income.

Social exclusion

A lack of access to resources, possessions and activities which most members of society take for granted, thereby affecting on individual's quality of life.

Welfare Reform Bill

An Act of Parliament that changes the law relating to social security benefits. It aims to make the benefit system fairer and better able to tackle poverty, worklessness and welfare dependency (through things such as promoting work and personal responsibility).

Assignments

Brainstorming

⇨ In small groups, discuss what you know about poverty.

- What is the meaning of the word poverty?
- What is fuel poverty?
- What is food poverty?
- What is a food bank?

Research

⇨ Design a Power Point presentation that will demonstrate what you have learnt about poverty, both in the UK and around the world. Consider the reasons why it is important to educate children and young adults about the implications of poverty, and what can be done to help those in need.

⇨ Using the article *What is poverty?* on page 1 draw up a weekly budget for a family of two adults and two children who are living in poverty. Work out how much money this family would spend on essential items such as food, transport, electricity and gas bills, then consider how much they would have left over for non-essential items such as entertainment.

⇨ Using the website www.localgiving.org research a local charity or community project in your area. Using this information, create a leaflet that presents information about your chosen organisation and explains to your classmates how they can get involved with charitable projects in your area.

⇨ Conduct a survey asking your classmates and parents about their perception of UK poverty and how they feel poverty impacts upon their lives, if at all. Using the statistics from this survey draw conclusions about poverty's impact in your area and detail the main concerns which you have discovered.

Design

⇨ Design a series of 30-second television advertisements aimed at raising public awareness of global poverty. Draw up a storyboard that informs the public about the implications of poverty.

⇨ Design an informative poster which raises awareness about fuel poverty – be sure to include some statistics! You might find 4.7 million people cannot afford to keep the lights on on page 8 helpful.

⇨ Design a poster which explains what the Global Goals are and how they will help eradicate poverty.

⇨ Choose one of the articles from this book and create an illustration that highlights the key themes of the piece.

Oral

⇨ In small groups, brainstorm about the meaning of the term 'poverty' and the impact it has upon people's lives. Make notes on your discussion and feedback to the rest of the class.

⇨ Devise a TV chat show with your classmates in order to discuss poverty in the UK. One pupil will play the role of an individual who struggles with relative poverty, another pupil will play a person who lives an affluent lifestyle and does not partake in charitable activities, and another will play a government minister who will discuss how government legislation tackles UK poverty. Other classmates will be the audience and will have the chance to ask questions to the interviewees. The audience should consider how each 'character' relates to the others, and potentially has an impact upon them and how poverty affects the different characters in various ways.

⇨ "The poor and hungry should not be punished for stealing food, but instead should be offered the help they need." Do you agree or disagree with this statement? Discuss in small groups and feedback to the class.

Reading/writing

⇨ Write a letter to your head teacher explaining why financial education at your school would be a good idea. You might want to include your own lesson plan ideas to help your school get started. Reading the article *Vulnerable young people intimidated by banks* on page 12 might be useful.

⇨ "More than six out of ten parents with household incomes of less than £25,000 are struggling to feed their children outside of term time according to crucial new research by Northumbria University." Read *Research reveals impact of the school holidays on struggling families* on page 17 and summarise the article in a blog post.

⇨ Read *Meet the kids scavenging on rubbish dumps to survive* on page 32. Imagine you are one of these young children forced to scavenge on rubbish dumps to survive and write a journal entry about your typical day and about why you do what you do.

⇨ Imagine that you represent a UK charity and compose a series of tweets which must be no more than 140 characters in length. The tweets should act as a series of hard-hitting messages which inform people about the effects of poverty in the UK and promote local community projects. You may also post links to external websites and photos which provide other information if you think this is helpful.

⇨ Go onto Trussell's Trust website, www.trusselltrust.org, and look at what they do. Write a review on what issues the charity focuses on, and how the organisation interacts with local communities in order to assist citizens who may be suffering with poverty and the implications that it brings. In your opinion, how successful has the organisation been in achieving their goals?

Acknowledgements

The publisher is grateful for permission to reproduce the material in this book. While every care has been taken to trace and acknowledge copyright, the publisher tenders its apology for any accidental infringement or where copyright has proved untraceable. The publisher would be pleased to come to a suitable arrangement in any such case with the rightful owner.

Images

All images courtesy of iStock.

Icons on pages 28 and 39 are made by Freepik from www.flaticon.com, except for the person profile on page 28 © Lucy G and the globe on page 30 © Zlatko Najdenovski.

Illustrations

Don Hatcher: pages 12. Simon Kneebone: pages 6 & 19. Angelo Madrid: pages 8 & 16.

Additional acknowledgements

Editorial on behalf of Independence Educational Publishers by Cara Acred.

With thanks to the Independence team: Mary Chapman, Sandra Dennis, Christina Hughes, Jackie Staines and Jan Sunderland.

Cara Acred

Cambridge

September 2016